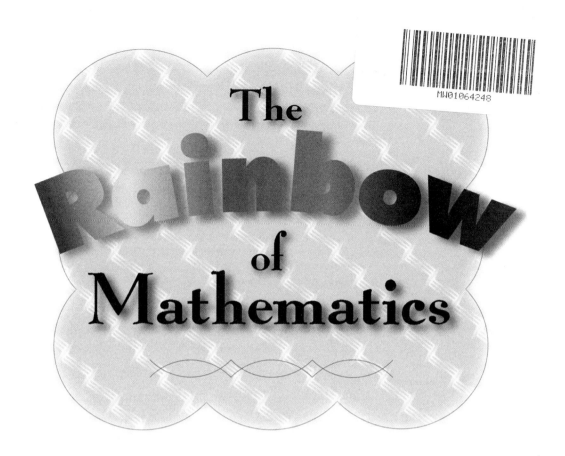

The Rainbow of Mathematics

A GEMS Handbook

by
Jaine Kopp
GEMS Mathematics
Curriculum Specialist
with
Lincoln Bergman

LHS GEMS
Great Explorations in Math and Science
Lawrence Hall of Science
University of California at Berkeley

The Lawrence Hall of Science (LHS) is a public science center on the University of California at Berkeley campus. LHS offers a full program of activities for the public. LHS is also a center for teacher education and curriculum research and development.

Initial support for the origination and publication of the GEMS series was provided by the A.W. Mellon Foundation and the Carnegie Corporation of New York. Under a grant from the National Science Foundation, GEMS Leader's Workshops have been held across the country. GEMS has also received support from: the McDonnell-Douglas Foundation and the McDonnell-Douglas Employee's Community Fund; the Employees Community Fund of Boeing California and the Boeing Corporation; the Hewlett Packard Company; the people at Chevron USA; the William K. Holt Foundation; Join Hands, the Health and Safety Educational Alliance; the Microscopy Society of America (MSA); the Shell Oil Company Foundation; and the Crail-Johnson Foundation. GEMS gratefully acknowledges the contribution of word processing equipment from Apple Computer, Inc. This support does not imply responsibility for statements or views expressed in publications of the GEMS program.

For information on GEMS leadership and professional development opportunities, to receive a free catalog and the *GEMS Network News,* or if you have any comments, criticism, and suggestions—all are welcomed—please write or call:

University of California, Berkeley
GEMS
Lawrence Hall of Science #5200
Berkeley, CA 94720-5200
(510) 642-7771
fax: (510) 643-0309
e-mail: gems@uclink4.berkeley.edu
web: www.lhs.berkeley.edu/GEMS

GEMS Staff

Principal Investigator: Glenn T. Seaborg
Director: Jacqueline Barber
Associate Director: Kimi Hosoume
Associate Director/Principal Editor: Lincoln Bergman
Mathematics Curriculum Specialist: Jaine Kopp
GEMS Network Director: Carolyn Willard
GEMS Workshop Coordinator: Laura Tucker
Staff Development Specialists: Lynn Barakos, Katharine Barrett, Kevin Beals, Ellen Blinderman, Beatrice Boffen, Gigi Dornfest, John Erickson, Stan Fukunaga, Philip Gonsalves, Linda Lipner, Karen Ostlund, Debra Sutter
Financial Assistant: Alice Olivier
Distribution Coordinator: Karen Milligan
Workshop Administrator: Terry Cort
Materials Manager: Vivian Tong
Distribution Representative: Felicia Roston
Shipping Assistant: Jodi Harskamp
Director of Marketing and Promotion: Matthew Osborn
Senior Editor: Carl Babcock
Editor: Florence Stone
Principal Publications Coordinator: Kay Fairwell
Art Director: Lisa Haderlie Baker
Senior Artists: Carol Bevilacqua, Rose Craig, Lisa Klofkorn
Staff Assistants: Larry Gates, Trina Huynh, Chastity Pérez, Dorian Traube

International Standard Book Number: 0-924886-18-8

What is GEMS?
Great Explorations in Math and Science

Students sorting and classifying buttons or leaves…waddling around like penguins on ice…exploring a strange green substance said to come from a distant planet…playing a math game from China or Africa…or solving a "crime" with chemistry. The basis for the GEMS approach is that students learn best by doing—an approach backed by overwhelming educational evidence. Activities first engage students in direct experience and experimentation, before introducing explanations of principles and concepts. Utilizing easily obtained and inexpensive materials, GEMS activities allow teachers without special background in science or mathematics to successfully present hands-on experiences.

Developed at the University of California at Berkeley's Lawrence Hall of Science, and tested in thousands of classrooms nationwide, more than 50 GEMS teacher's guides offer a wide spectrum of learning opportunities from preschool through tenth grade.

Emphasis on teamwork and cooperative learning, the use of a wide variety of learning formats, and reliance on direct experience rather than textbooks makes GEMS highly appropriate for use with populations that have been historically underrepresented in science and mathematics pursuits and careers. In GEMS activities, students are encouraged to work together to discover more, explore a problem, or solve a mystery, rather than fixating on the so-called right answer, or engaging in negatively competitive behavior. Cooperative (or collaborative) learning is one of the most effective strategies for bridging and appreciating differences and diversities of background and culture. It is also one of the most effective ways to help prepare students for the workplaces of the future.

The GEMS series interweaves a number of educational ideas and goals. GEMS units strongly support the inquiry-driven, activity-based approach to science and mathematics education. and spell out how that approach can be practically presented, by veteran and inexperienced teachers, to the enormous benefit of all students. GEMS guides encompass important learning objectives, summarized on the front page of each guide under the headings of skills, concepts, themes, mathematics strands, and aspects that relate to the nature of science and mathematics. These objectives can be directly and flexibly related to national standards and benchmarks, other science and mathematics curricula, state frameworks, and district guidelines.

Since classroom testing began in 1984, more than 700,000 teachers and at least ten million students have taken part in GEMS activities. In collaboration with thousands of teachers, GEMS activities are adapted for the classroom, for use by teachers who may not have special background in math and science. A rapidly expanding national network of teachers and educators take part in GEMS Leader's and Associate's workshops and receive a free national newsletter, the *GEMS Network News*. There are now more than 50 GEMS Centers or Network Sites nationwide, in many regions of the country, and internationally, providing support to teachers in their regions through workshops and diverse professional development opportunities. GEMS is a growing series. New guides and handbooks are being developed constantly and current guides are revised frequently. We welcome your comments and letters. Let us hear from you.

Acknowledgments

For some years, mathematics educators at the Lawrence Hall of Science (LHS) have used the metaphor of a rainbow to communicate the interweaving strands of mathematics. Their presentations have been flexibly modified based on the needs of the audience, developments and trends in mathematics education at the time, and presenter preferences. Among past and present LHS-based mathematics educators who deserve acknowledgment for their contributions to the "early light" of rainbow-as-math-metaphor are Ruth Cossey, Paul Giganti, Linda Lipner, and Elizabeth Stage. They trace its origin to Donna Goldenstein, a teacher in Hayward, who developed it for the first Bay Area Mathematics Project "Road Show." Former GEMS Mathematics Curriculum Specialist Jan M. Goodman further contributed to its refinement and presentation. The metaphor has also been used and adapted by mathematics educators from the LHS EQUALS and Family Math programs and has been presented during a number of LHS summer professional development institutes such as the NSF-sponsored PRISM institute during the mid-1990s.

Most recently, the "Rainbow of Mathematics" has become a special feature of Great Explorations in Math and Science (GEMS) professional development efforts. The author of this handbook, Jaine Kopp, GEMS Mathematics Curriculum Specialist, has frequently presented it at GEMS Associate's Workshops and other teacher education venues. Over the past several years, Jaine has sought to align the GEMS math rainbow with standards and trends in mathematics education, while retaining aspects that are unique to the GEMS approach. Jaine has also brought this valuable perspective to the process of developing new GEMS guides and to correlating GEMS with national mathematics standards and other leading guidelines for excellence. As this handbook began to materialize, a series of meetings on GEMS and mathematics were held with Jaine that included GEMS Director Jacqueline Barber, former GEMS Science Curriculum Specialist Cary Sneider, GEMS Network Director Carolyn Willard, and GEMS Associate Directors Kimi Hosoume and Lincoln Bergman. Lincoln Bergman assisted in rewriting and editing this handbook for publication and Carolyn Willard reviewed successive versions, even as she too began presenting "The Rainbow of Mathematics" at GEMS workshops nationwide.

We are especially appreciative of the reviews of semi-final versions of the handbook by Beverly Braxton, José Franco, Phil Gonsalves, Carol Langbort, Karen Mayfield-Ingram, Karen Ostlund, Steven Rakow, Elizabeth Stage, Dick Stanley, and Virginia Thompson. While we have attempted to incorporate their comments where possible, final responsibility for all aspects rests with the GEMS program. We revise our publications frequently and welcome your comments, which will be carefully considered for upcoming editions. ■

Table of Contents

The Rainbow of Math

by Lincoln Bergman

Math is a rainbow
Colorful arc
Numbers our days
Measurement's mark
Lines, shapes, and rays,
Light up the dark

The rainbow of math
Glows everywhere
Finding solutions
How many are there?
Making predictions
Dividing fair share

Math is a rainbow
Logic is sought
Real-world connection
Thinking is taught
Open your eyes
To what math hath wrought!

The rainbow of math
Can shine inspiration
But as taught in the past
Often led to frustration
Math comes to life
Through cooperation.

Math is a rainbow
A pot of gold path
High in a plane
Or taking a bath
It all is a part of
The beauty of math.

The rainbow of math
Is far from archaic
Nor are its mysteries
Dull or prosaic
Unknowns are revealed
In realms algebraic.

Math is a rainbow
Though sometimes discrete
It can bring things together
On everyone's street
On train of tomorrow
Math has a front seat!

The rainbow of math
Dawn of the new
Surfing the internet
E-mailing too
Who knows what the tools
Of the future will do?

Math is a rainbow
Blooms like a flower
Shines understanding
After rain shower
All students can
Acquire math power!

The true spirit of delight, the exaltation . . . which is the touchstone of the highest excellence, is to be found in mathematics as surely as in poetry.

Bertrand Russell, Mysticism and Logic, *1917*

Introduction

This handbook features a presentation entitled "The Rainbow of Mathematics" that has been presented frequently at GEMS workshops for teachers, teacher educators, and administrators. Using the visual metaphor of a rainbow, it summarizes the main ideas and current approaches in content-rich mathematics education. It is written as a script, but there is no requirement that presenters use exactly the same words. In fact, we strongly recommend and assume that you would want to adapt it for your own particular audience, providing examples of your own, using your own language, and varying the length and sophistication depending on circumstance. We have prepared our sample script at a fairly basic level, to serve as a framework for adaptation. We include some presentation tips in the back of the book based on our experience.

"Teaching mathematics is a complex endeavor, and there are no easy recipes."

NCTM, *Principles and Standards for School Mathematics*, page 17.

Connection to the NCTM

Serving a nationwide audience, GEMS uses national standards in content areas to guide our development of curriculum resources; in the case of mathematics, we look to the National Council of Teachers of Mathematics (NCTM). In 1989, NCTM published the *Curriculum and Evaluation Standards for School Mathematics* followed by the *Professional Standards for Teaching Mathematics* in 1991. Together these documents guided mathematics education and our development of mathematics resources for teachers. In 2000, the NCTM published *Principles and Standards for School Mathematics*. This document blended the contents of the two earlier standards and describes a vision of mathematics education that includes: principles for school mathematics; standards for mathematics education for grades P/K through grade 12; and the steps to move toward the vision of these *Principles and Standards*.

Within our metaphor, the *Principles and Standards* are represented by the various elements of a rainbow. The Mathematics Standards are represented by the arcs of the rainbow and the sun rays, with some modifications. We have called the mathematics content standards "strands" and further subdivided some standards. For example, in the presentation script, we make Statistics and Probability two separate strands as well as separate Discrete Mathematics as its own strand. These content standards are meant to be taught across the grade levels with different emphases varying between grade levels. The sun rays in the rainbow represent the process standards and are identical to the ones in the NCTM Standards. In addition, we have added Pattern to these sun rays as pattern runs through all of mathematics.

The Principles and Standards for School Mathematics *address the following overarching themes: Equity; Curriculum; Teaching; Learning; Assessment; and Technology. The Mathematics Standards for all grade levels include: (1) Number and Operation; (2) Algebra; (3) Geometry; (4) Measurement; (5) Data Analysis and Probability; (6) Problem Solving; (7) Reasoning and Proof; (8) Communication; (9) Connections; and (10) Representation.*

The Principles outline the features of high-quality mathematics education and are important pieces of the rainbow. The Equity principle (excellence and high expectations for all students) is represented through our "pots of gold." The Curriculum (coherent, focused on important math and articulated across grade levels) and Teaching (supporting and challenging students) principles are represented in the "raindrops," labelled Discourse and Real World Problems and Investigations. The Learning principle (build deeper understanding from experience and prior knowledge) is also represented by two raindrops—Collaboration and Discourse. The Assessment principle (support the learning and inform the teacher and students) is the Authentic Assessment raindrop. Finally, the Technology principle is represented by a raindrop labelled Tools. Not only does this raindrop represent electronic technologies, it also represents tools, such as pattern blocks and measurement materials, to gain concrete understanding.

Presentation of the Rainbow of Mathematics

Though this rainbow serves our purpose to make connections to the national standards and principles, presenters have varied the metaphor in many other ways. It can be adapted for state or district frameworks. It can also be used to articulate the features of a curriculum series. There are many other rainbow variations. We encourage you to use the one that best suits your needs.

During the presentation, we use a set of overheads—made from the masters in the back of the book (pp. 52–55)—as the visual elements to build and communicate the metaphor. Beginning with the first arcs of the rainbow (mathematics content) and continuing with the raindrops (principles and implementation tools), then the Sun with its rays (process standards) and finally the pots of gold (equity), the elements are explained and come together to portray a rich mathematics education program.

Some presenters use a large felt board with felt pieces for all of the elements in the rainbow metaphor—arcs, raindrops, the sun and its rays, and pots of gold. You could make your own rainbow-of-math felt board. Alternately, you could present these via Powerpoint or similar presentation formats.

This "Rainbow of Mathematics" presentation can also be adapted for presentation to parents, community groups, administrators, and other involved citizens and organizations. It will hopefully serve as a useful tool to help provide these key audiences with understandable information on the new developments in mathematics education. In turn, this understanding can help gain their support and advocacy for the resources and changes necessary in our educational system for the rainbow vision to truly be achieved. We welcome your comments and suggestions.

The "M" in GEMS

From the start, the Great Explorations in Math and Science (GEMS) program has sought to live up to its name by having a strong mathematical component. As the series began to take shape, GEMS began to make real strides toward the twin goals of: (1) Having a significant number of GEMS guides with a central mathematics focus; and (2) Providing exciting and practical experiences for students that integrate mathematics and science.

In order to address and strengthen the ways that the GEMS series meets these twin goals, there are a growing number of GEMS guides that concentrate on mathematics—including *Build It! Festival, Frog Math, Group Solutions, Group Solutions, Too!, In All Probability, Math Around the World, Math on the Menu, QUADICE,* and *Treasure Boxes.* Two new guides on algebra for upper and lower elementary students are under development. Both *Group Solutions* and *Group Solutions, Too!* have as their central focus cooperative logic which bridges both mathematical and scientific reasoning. GEMS Leaders and Associates nationwide have told us that the mathematics-centered GEMS guides have been especially successful in reaching teachers who might otherwise not have ventured into an activity-based approach. They tell us that the activities convince even reluctant teachers that hands-on, inquiry-based learning can be effective, content-rich, practical, and fun. We hope that the GEMS units are making a modest contribution to helping a new generation of students have successful experiences in mathematics.

As the number of GEMS guides increased, the examples of exciting and practical integration of math and science also grew. *Height-O-Meters* uses the principles of triangulation to measure the height of a flagpole—this measuring technique is then used to calculate the heights of model rockets in *Experimenting with Model Rockets.* When students investigate fingerprints in the *Fingerprinting* guide, they are examining real-world examples of patterns that they sort and classify, and then they apply this knowledge and use their problem-solving skills to solve a mystery related to fingerprints. This is a clear example of math and science walking hand in hand. Many of the GEMS guides for early childhood, such as *Eggs Eggs Everywhere*, *Ladybugs*, and *Mother Opossum and Her Babies*, have very strong mathematical components. Other science-oriented guides with prominent mathematics connections include *Bubble-ology, Discovering Density, Paper Towel Testing, Vitamin C Testing, Investigating Artifacts, More Than Magnifiers*, and *Moons of Jupiter*—to name only a few. In fact, almost all the "science" guides naturally interweave many mathematical elements, including graphing, sorting, classification, measurement with non-standard and standard units, logical reasoning, statistical analysis, chemical formulas, geometrical structures of the natural and constructed world, and much more.

In many respects, too sharp a distinction between mathematics and science does an inaccurate disservice to both. Many of the key elements in strong mathematics programs are also embedded in science programs. For example, reasoning, problem solving, and communication are crucial to mathematics. The many strategies and skills that are used to arrive at solutions and the need to explain one's thinking and reasoning are as important in science— and many areas of the curriculum—as in mathematics. Many real-world careers involve both science and mathematics, and there is a growing realization that our teaching and learning need to reflect the integration of science and mathematics.

In 2000, the GEMS series received the award for "Excellence in Integrating Science and Mathematics" from the School Science and Mathematics Association (SSMA).

Mathematics Opens Doors
There can be no doubt that basic and diverse branches of mathematical learning and related content, skills, capabilities, and reasoning are vitally important for the future career choices and life directions of our students.

Yet ask a roomful of adults to think back to their days in school, specifically to think about their memories of learning math, and you are likely to hear lots of moans and groans. Ask for more detail and you may hear statements like: "I remember pages and pages of drills—addition, subtraction, multiplication and division; I remember timed tests; memorizing multiplication tables; getting 'the' right answer; not being able to think quickly enough and remember number facts." Many people will say they have "math anxiety."

Teachers, and all people, tend to teach in the same way they were taught, unless they have new and repeated experiences that assist them to come to a new level of understanding. Mathematics in particular not only suffers from having been taught in ineffective and uninteresting ways in the past, it also is associated with a range of phobias and stereotypes. The class nerd (formerly with slide rule) and the wild-haired professor scribbling complex formulas on the chalkboard are two stereotypical and intimidating images that come to mind.

Hypatia, *worked on the geometry of conic sections; also a scientist and astronomer*

Maria Guetana Agnesi, *mathematician and physicist known for her work on the reversed sine curve*

Historically, in most societies, mathematics has been viewed as a male domain. Even so, there have been extraordinary contributions to the field made by women—from ancient times to the present. In recent years, some real progress has been made—many more women have received advanced degrees in mathematics and related fields and some have become professors. Although they are not yet equally recognized or rewarded, women in far greater numbers are entering and excelling in many professions that require advanced education in science and mathematics.

Sonya Kovalevsky — *the Cuachy-Kovalevsky Theorem of partial differential equations.*

Mathematics has been a major social and class "divisor" as well. Old-style and continuing practices of racial and cultural segregation and economic class tracking, while no longer as overt or socially acceptable, still take their toll and unfortunately remain *de facto* in many communities. Parent's organizations, coalitions of educators, and other organizations, such as the Mathematics, Engineering, Science Achievement (MESA) program and the Algebra Project, have formed in recent years to correct and repair these injustices, and to develop programs to ensure that all students have access to higher learning in math and science.

Many studies have shown that experience and training in mathematics is in fact **the key** to whether or not students go on to take more advanced courses in high school and college, and is a primary indicator of their career potential and achievement. In this sense, mathematics takes on social, economic, and political importance far greater than most people realize. It is to the credit of many math educators and mathematicians that they have realized their responsibility to transform mathematics education. In this sense, for all of our students, mathematics can be seen as a key to their future. It opens doors that otherwise remain closed.

At the Lawrence Hall of Science (LHS), mathematics educators from the EQUALS and Family Math programs have long been in the forefront of efforts nationwide and internationally to place mathematics education on a new footing of equality. Other LHS mathematics education programs and educators from these programs have been active in devising teacher networks and inservice programs to help teachers relearn key aspects of mathematics content and pedagogy to inform their practice—in order to better serve all students. It was from among these educators that the vision of mathematics education as a rainbow first emerged.

The NCTM *Principles and Standards for School Mathematics*, as well as the *National Science Education Standards, Benchmarks for Science Literacy,* and many state frameworks and district guidelines, share a common, egalitarian vision—that mathematics and science learning opportunities should be available to **all** students, regardless of gender, background or heritage, physical or learning challenge.

Great Explorations in Math and Science fits nicely into this vision and GEMS units have been consciously designed to reach and challenge all students. Because GEMS units are designed, tested, and continually revised to be used effectively by teachers who may not have special background in math or science, they lend themselves to the goal of reaching all students. Because GEMS activities require only easily-accessible materials they can be presented successfully with limited budgets. The emphasis on teamwork and cooperative learning in GEMS activities has been shown to be one of the most successful strategies in assisting students and teachers to both bridge and positively appreciate differences and diversities.

In fact, through GEMS and many other fine mathematics and science programs, mathematics can become dynamic and powerful, colorful and imaginative. That is one of the reasons we have chosen a rainbow, a spectrum of color, to represent the beauty and power of modern mathematical learning. ■

ACHIEVING BALANCE—A POLITICAL NOTE

Several reviewers of this handbook pointed out that in some locales and with some audiences, a presentation such as "The Rainbow of Mathematics" may activate local concerns about mathematical achievement. Specifically, in some communities and states, more innovative activity-based approaches have been criticized by those who believe in traditional teaching approaches. Traditionalists argue that teaching basic skills should be at the core of mathematics programs— what was needed in the past is still needed today. Proponents of the reform movement contend that rote learning with an emphasis on skill building does not develop conceptual understanding or problem-solving skills—what failed to work in the past for many students will still fail to work today. Reform-minded educators agree that students do need to develop and learn basic skills; however, they also see the need for students to develop critical thinking abilities so that they can apply their skills to non-routine problems. The debate is exacerbated when test scores fall below par. If a reform curriculum had been in place, the traditionalists will point to the low scores and call for a "back to basics" program. Likewise, if a traditional program had been in place when the scores go down, the reformers will point to the tendency for students to memorize with no under-standing as the culprit and call for programmatic changes. Each group is inclined to blame the other for poor performance—often before enough time has elapsed to truly evaluate what students have learned! This further polarizes the two groups and provides more fuel for the debate. Though traditionally math-ematics education in the United States has concentrated on skills, and reformers have emphasized problem solving as the antidote, neither approach provides the balance that strong mathematics programs need. The common ground would be to create mathematics programs that include a balance of skills, concepts, and problem solving. You should be prepared to address these issues by finding out about the character of this debate in your region and becoming acquainted with any evidence about student achievement that may support a call for a balanced program for all students.

...AND SOME WISE WORDS FROM THE PAST

"It is not the purpose of this book to teach number facts to the primary student. Education is development, and especially this is true of the best primary work. The mind of the child just entering school is bent upon investigation, exploration, and discovery. It is the privilege of the primary teacher to guide this investigation, furnish a proper and fruitful environment for exploration, and teach the child the use of the best written and spoken language in which he may tell of his discoveries."

Della Van Amburgh
First Days in Number
A Primer of Arithmetic
**Silver Burdett and Company,
New York, Boston, Chicago** 1903

*T*oday I'd like to share with you the rainbow metaphor we use to represent a mathematics education program at its best—we call it "The Rainbow of Mathematics."

Most likely some of you, just hearing me use the word "mathematics," have already begun a mental groan or felt a shiver of fear run down your spine! Before we travel over the rainbow, think back to when you went to school— what were your math experiences like? What images and feelings are stirred up? *(Accept a number of brief responses that range from negative experiences such as finding the "right" answer, computational work, memorizing rules and formulas, difficult to understand, lectures, etc. to more positive comments such as great teachers, meaningful problem solving, it made sense, I loved the beauty of geometry, etc.)*

Many of us remember number work that included lots of rote drills, timed tests, multiplication tables, long division, and so on. If we look back to the 1950s, mastery of those number skills prepared students for such jobs as cashiers and bookkeepers. In today's technological world, many career directions and decisions everyone makes in daily life demand mathematical capability that definitely includes, but also extends well beyond, basic computation skills.

Most of us remember learning formulas and standard approaches to solving problems. There was a "right" answer to each of the repetitive problems posed. Our teachers had the active role of "downloading" information to passive students. It was an alien thought to have students work together to solve a problem—that was considered cheating! As students move into today's work force, they need to take with them the ability to work collaboratively and solve complex problems.

Times have changed since we went to school. The mathematics that all our students need to be successful in their future pursuits has changed as well. Our mathematics programs need to reflect these changes to develop mathematically powerful students. Today, using the metaphor of a rainbow, we are going to create a bright vision for mathematics education. Let's start with the colorful arcs of the rainbow.

NUMBER
Place the first felt rainbow arc labeled "Number" in the middle of the felt board.

As we've said, what most people remember about mathematics is a lot of number work that came in the form of repetitive exercises, rote drill and the like—which, in fact, was not really mathematics but arithmetic. Once mastered, a person had computational skills. Many people refer to these as "basic skills." Computational skills are still an important part of every student's tool kit. However, the way that students acquire these skills today is likely to be very different than in the past. Today, students need to understand what numbers mean and how the operations work. They need to be taught in the context of problems that are meaningful and understandable to them. Estimation, mental math, place value, fractions, percentages, and decimals, and number theory are all part of this important strand.

"Historically, number has been a cornerstone of the mathematics curriculum."

NCTM, *Principles and Standards for School Mathematics*, page 32.

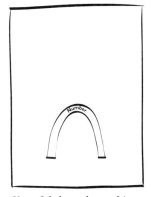

Your felt board graphic would look like this (above). If you are using overheads, the rainbow is not built strand by strand, so you would display the first overhead during the entire discussion of mathematics content (below).

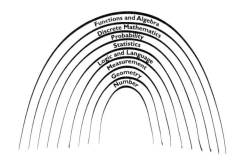

"Developing fluency [with numbers] requires a balance and a connection between conceptual understanding and computational proficiency." NCTM, *Principles and Standards for School Mathematics*, page 35.

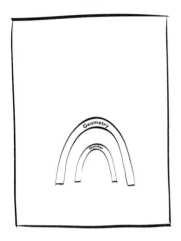

You may need to explain briefly that a tessellation is a tiled pattern of polygons or other shapes that exactly fills a flat surface with no overlapping or gaps between the shapes (such a tiled floor or counter). The artist M. C. Escher created tessellations in many of his designs. Topology is the study of the properties of shapes and figures that relates to what happens when the shapes or figures are bent, stretched, or molded. A topologist may study a surface or a solid, a pretzel or a cylinder, a doughnut or a map, such as a relief map. The GEMS teacher's guide Build It! Festival *has tessellation activities, and the GEMS exhibit guide* Shapes, Loops, & Images *includes both tessellations and some challenging topological puzzles.*

We also need to recognize that well beyond the role it plays in computation, number plays a very basic and integral role in all of mathematics, science, and many other fields. Numbers are quantifiers—they tell us how much and how many. Numbers are the root of our base 10 system. Numbers allow mathematical information to be communicated—from the data on a graph to the probability of rolling a seven with two dice. In addition, students need access to technological tools, including calculators and computers, to explore number concepts. Number is a very important part of our rainbow and, as we'll see, it is interwoven throughout all of the strands, but mathematics is also much more than number.

Let's continue creating the rainbow by adding

GEOMETRY

Place felt arc labeled "Geometry" as the next arc in the rainbow on the felt board.

Geometry connects us to the real world. Everything has a shape or a form that is either two- or three-dimensional. If we look around this room, we can see many examples of geometric shapes. What are some shapes you see around you? *(Take a few responses.)*

We recognize these shapes because they are defined by their attributes. For example, if I asked you to visualize a square, do you have an image? We all know and recognize squares because we've had many experiences with them—we know the definition of square as a closed shape with four equal sides and four 90° angles. *(If there is time, you could instead ask the audience, "What are special characteristics of squares?" Take a few responses,)*

Many of us may remember geometry from high school when we did two-column proofs. Though creating proofs is one part of geometry, in which convincing arguments prove statements, there are other ways to explain geometric insights. Today, we know it is important for geometry to begin much earlier than high school. From the start of their education, students need to do explorations in geometry. Starting with hands-on experiences in early grades that are connected to the real world, the explorations lead to development of a geometric vocabulary that is used and built on throughout the mathematics education program. In this way, students have a solid foundation for more advanced geometry in later grades.

Students need opportunities to investigate the essence of geometry—the exploration of points, angles, lines, and planes. Their investigations can take them into such areas as symmetry, tessellations, topology, spatial visualization, and more. Geometry connects mathematics to other disciplines including art and architecture, geology and chemistry. Geometry also relates very closely to the next part of a rich mathematical program, which is:

MEASUREMENT

Place felt arc labeled "Measurement" as the next arc in the rainbow on the felt board.

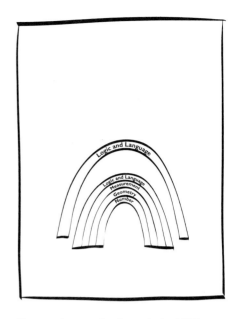

Measurement interweaves naturally with both number and geometry. When we described the square earlier, we needed to talk about the number of degrees in each of its four angles as well as the length of each of its four sides. Without those measurement criteria, our polygon would not necessarily be a square! Linear and angular measurements connect geometry to measurement.

Do you use measurement every day? Absolutely! Whoever cooks (or orders take-out!) needs to know how much is needed to feed themselves and their family. Everyone who drives a car knows how far they can go when the gas gauge gets close to "E." Measurement begins with comparisons—What is longer? How much longer? or Which is heavier? How much heavier? To help describe these type of comparisons, units of measure come into play. At first, familiar, non-standard units of measure, such as blocks or paper clips, provide the necessary tools to measure. Using these tools provides younger students with experiences to understand the concept of measurement and units of measure.

Later, standard systems of units, such as the metric system and those of time, weight, etc., are used and enable students to make measurements. Units are also used in combination to find measures of other properties as they solve problems related to area, density, and acceleration.

Measuring also involves more than simply using a tool and coming up with a number for an answer. It involves making decisions about the accuracy of the measurement and interpreting that number.

Measurement is used in all occupations and in everyday life. Just think, without measurement, we would all be arriving at work at various times, we wouldn't be able to duplicate recipes or experiments, or be able to buy a pound of our favorite cookies at the bakery shop!

This next arc of the rainbow
LOGIC and LANGUAGE
is also used by all of us on a daily basis.
Place felt arc labeled "Logic and Language" as the next arc in the rainbow on the felt board.

Simply defined, logic is a fundamental thinking skill that allows us to make sense out of things—whether it involves an everyday situation or a complex mathematical problem. Logical thinking skills help us organize our thoughts, plan strategies, and solve problems. The ability to think clearly and to reason logically is an especially vital life skill given the complexity of today's society and world.

If your audience is familiar with the GEMS guide Mother Opossum and Her Babies, *you can use the measurement activities as an example of using non-standard units.*

"Understanding that all measurements are approximations is a difficult but important concept for students." NCTM, *Principles and Standards for School Mathematics,* page 46.

If your audience is familiar with the GEMS guide Math Around the World, *you can use an example of logic as applied to the games in that guide.*

"Learning how to choose an appropriate unit is a major part of understanding measurement." NCTM, *Principles and Standards for School Mathematics,* page 45.

At the primary level, we need to start building students' logical thinking skills and develop their repertoire of problem-solving strategies. An essential building block that starts students thinking logically is sorting and classifying. Similarly, looking for patterns and finding relationships also leads to higher-level thinking skills. As students increase their reasoning powers, and develop inductive and deductive reasoning abilities, they acquire a set of tools. These tools enable students to solve traditional problems that require linear, sequential thinking—like those computational problems we talked about earlier. But even more importantly, students become able to solve problems that require the use of a variety of skills and strategies. Their ability to think in divergent ways allows them to tackle complex problems.

Many problems have multiple solutions, so there are different ways to approach and solve each problem. Beyond solving the problem, it is very important that students be able to explain and articulate the logic and reasoning behind their solutions. We know that a student has fully grasped how to solve a problem when she is able to communicate the process and solution to others. People often realize they haven't fully understood something until asked to explain it to someone else. Being able to explain a concept or our own thinking really lets us know we understand it.

By its very nature, the strand of logic and language intersects with all the other strands and areas of the curriculum such as science, writing, social studies, and literature. In mathematics, students need to use their logical thinking and reasoning skills to solve problems and explain solutions— whether it be to a geometric proof or determining how many pennies are needed to create a stack as high as students are tall. And those logical thinking skills certainly come into play as we add the next area of mathematics to our rainbow…

STATISTICS

Place felt arc labeled "Statistics" as the next arc in the rainbow on the felt board.

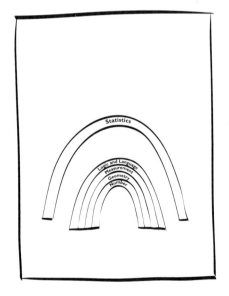

Two units for young students, Sifting Through Science *and* Treasure Boxes, *make use of concrete graphs to develop a foundation for understanding statistics.*

"Students should learn what it means to make valid statistical comparisons."
NCTM, *Principles and Standards for School Mathematics,* page 50.

Think about all the places we see statistics. *(If time permits, ask participants for some examples of where we see statistics in daily life.)* From the cereal box on the breakfast table to the sports pages in the daily newspaper, from television commercials to opinion polls, we are presented with information in the form of data. Sometimes such data are presented in a straightforward way that can be easily interpreted, but at other times the organization of the data may lead us to make inferences that are not necessarily true! For example, in advertising, a flurry of data may be presented to convince us that a particular product is the best, even though it may not be significantly better than its competition. We need to use our critical thinking skills to determine the validity of the data, and to evaluate how the information is presented and interpreted.

To help students develop the skills to evaluate and interpret statistics, they first need experience with data—collecting, organizing, and making sense out of it. This process begins with students creating concrete graphs—

graphs that use real materials. Even at an early level, students should be expected to learn the difference between making true statements about the data on the graph and making inferences from the data. For example, on a shoe graph, the observed fact that there are more tie shoes than other types of shoe is a true statement, while saying that tie shoes are the most popular kind of shoe is an inference. It is also important to organize the same data—such as the shoes—in more than one way to see how the organization impacts the graph's interpretation—both the true statements and inferences.

From directed class activities, students learn how to gather and organize data on their own in a variety of forms. With experience, they can determine the best ways to represent the data. In addition, they can evaluate data from newspapers, advertisements, opinion polls, science experiments, and social studies classes. These experiences will sharpen their critical thinking skills and prepare them to examine graphs and statistics before jumping to conclusions about what is being represented. As they further develop an understanding of statistics and can analyze numerical data, they will acquire key capabilities to evaluate issues and make important decisions in an informed way.

The work of many professionals depends on statistics such as stockbrokers, insurance underwriters, public health workers, educators, city planners, product developers, etc. The next arc of the rainbow often depends upon statistics and also has many real-life connections.

PROBABILITY

Place felt arc labeled "Probability" as the next arc in the rainbow on the felt board. (If participants are familiar with the GEMS guide *In All Probability*, use examples from that unit.)

"Chances are" that you've all had life experience with probability. Probability is the likelihood of an event occurring, the chance that something will or will not happen. When you toss a penny, how many outcomes are there? Yes, two—you can get either a head or a tail. So there are two possible outcomes. What is the likelihood of getting a head? That's right, "1 out of 2" or 50%. This is called the "theoretical" probability of this event happening. Now, if we conduct a probability experiment and actually start flipping the penny, will we always get exactly five heads and five tails in ten tosses? No, not necessarily. The more times we flip, the more likely we'll approximate that 1 out of 2 probability, but we're also very likely to get somewhat more heads than tails, or vice versa! We can record all of our flips, then analyze that data to see what happened in our experiment and how closely our experiment came to the theoretical probability.

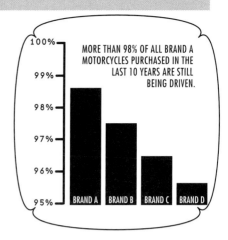

This graph from the GEMS unit In All Probability *is used as an instructional tool to help students see how data can be represented to try to convince consumers of a particular product's superiority.*

The theoretical probability can be expressed as $P \text{ (heads)} = \frac{1}{2}$.

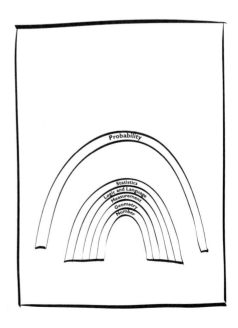

Probability also has to do with prediction. Predictions are guesses—sometimes they can be "wild" guesses, while other times we use prior knowledge to make a more "educated" guess. In many professions, educated guesses play a large role in the work people do. Meteorologists make predictions about our weather, epidemiologists predict the course of outbreaks of illnesses, and seismologists gather data that may help predict future earthquakes. In each of these fields, data are gathered and analyzed to predict future occurrences. In our own lives, we make predictions—such as what candidate will win an election or whether our favorite sports team will win a game.

Students begin to understand probability by conducting probability experiments—often in the form of games that use coins, spinners, and dice. They predict winners and judge whether the game is fair. From these experiences, they gain an intuitive understanding of probability. As they further investigate the game by collecting and analyzing data, they develop a numerical understanding of the probability. Going back to the penny flip, primary students can conduct a penny toss experiment and make predictions of outcomes that gives them an intuitive understanding about probability, while upper elementary students can play a two-coin toss game and determine if it is fair or not based on data they collect. Older students can go further and examine the theoretical probability of dice games to determine the fairness of the games.

Probability is closely connected with both statistics and number. In addition, because there are finite, countable numbers of outcomes that can be generated when determining probabilities, it also connects closely to the next area of mathematics...

DISCRETE MATHEMATICS
Place felt arc labeled "Discrete Mathematics" as the next arc in the rainbow on the felt board.

Though discrete mathematics includes a wide variety of topics and has many applications in everyday life, it is often an area of math that seems hard to grasp. However, without even knowing that is what they are doing, many teachers do discrete mathematics problems with their students on a regular basis!

The word discrete means separate and distinct. In mathematics, when we think of discrete, it means separate and countable quantities versus continuous quantities. To help understand what we mean by that, here are a few real-world examples: think about using sugar cubes—each cube is separate and countable vs. pouring honey which flows and is continuous; or going down steps vs. going down a slide; counting rainy days vs. measuring seasonal rainfall; the peas and carrots on your plate vs. the mashed potatoes! We could come up with a long list, but let's move on to further explore this branch of mathematics.

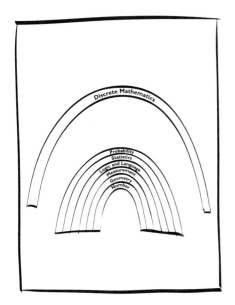

Ask the participants by a show of hands how many have heard of discrete mathematics. Then ask what they have heard about it. Take a few responses.

Let's start with one area that many people are familiar with—systematic listing and counting. Here's a problem to help illustrate this. If you had three hats and four pairs of sunglasses, how many different combinations of one hat and one pair of glasses could you create?

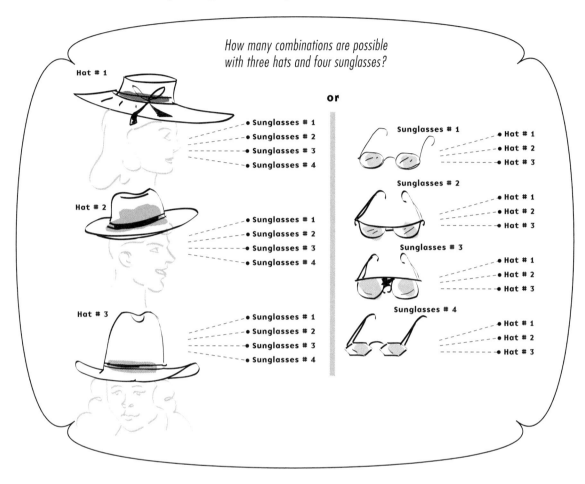

How many combinations are possible with three hats and four sunglasses?

Hat # 1

or

• Sunglasses # 1
• Sunglasses # 2
• Sunglasses # 3
• Sunglasses # 4

Sunglasses # 1
• Hat # 1
• Hat # 2
• Hat # 3

Hat # 2

• Sunglasses # 1
• Sunglasses # 2
• Sunglasses # 3
• Sunglasses # 4

Sunglasses # 2
• Hat # 1
• Hat # 2
• Hat # 3

Sunglasses # 3
• Hat # 1
• Hat # 2
• Hat # 3

Hat # 3

• Sunglasses # 1
• Sunglasses # 2
• Sunglasses # 3
• Sunglasses # 4

Sunglasses # 4
• Hat # 1
• Hat # 2
• Hat # 3

You may want to have sunglasses and hats available to concretely do this problem. Have a participant come up and select one hat and one pair of glasses. Ask how many more combinations they can create. Listen to their strategies for determining the total number. Ask if there is a countable number.   [There are 12.]

Yes, this is a countable number and there are many ways to arrive at it. However, approaching the problem in an organized way, such as using a list, chart, or diagram will ensure that you find all the possibilities. This aspect of discrete mathematics uses counting principles and is known as combinatorics, which includes combinations and permutations.

Discrete mathematics also includes graph theory which uses models to analyze data in separate, countable ways. Graphs and other diagrams can show the ways that groups of objects are both separate from each other and also intersect or have some attributes in common. Some real-world examples are travel routes, such as those of airplanes or mail carriers; schedules for committees or tournaments; or assigning office space in a workplace or frequencies to radio stations. Let's look at one specific problem. Given 16 college basketball teams, set up a tournament schedule that uses single elimination to determine the winner. To solve this problem, a diagram can be drawn to determine the number of games necessary as well as who will play whom throughout the tournament.

Here is one diagram to represent the tournament schedule:

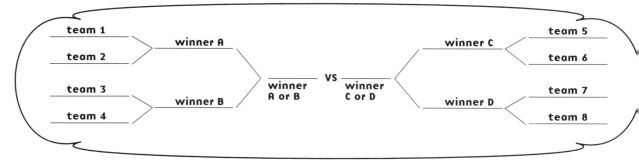

Another important part of discrete mathematics involves looking for an optimal solution. Here's an example of this sort of problem in a real-world context. You've parked your car in a garage where they "stack" vehicles to fit the maximum number in the given space. You arrive back sooner than expected, and the attendant needs to move cars to get to yours which, of course, is boxed in. What is the most efficient way—or the minimal number of moves—for the attendant to get your car out? So you can see that discrete mathematics is not really so "discreet"—it plays a role in our daily lives. As we understand it better, we can often identify it as part of the mathematics we are already doing.

Let's add the next strand to our rainbow…

FUNCTIONS and ALGEBRA
Place felt arc labeled "Functions and Algebra" as the next arc in the rainbow on the felt board.

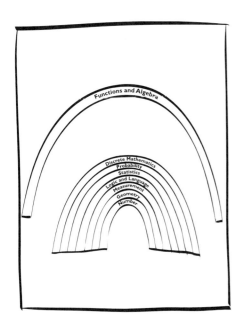

Functions:
Most simply defined, functions are relationships. By formal definition, a function is a mapping of all the members of one set to the members in another. Let's look at a function—the relationship between the number of people and their total number of eyes. Taking the people in this room, one person has two eyes, two people have four eyes, etc. This is a proportional relationship…1 to 2. By discerning it, we can determine how many eyes the people in this room have. Also, by articulating it as a function, we can determine how many eyes "x" number of people would have.
$[F(x) = 2x)]$

"All students should learn algebra."
NCTM, *Principles and Standards for School Mathematics,* page 37.

As we teach functions, it is important to look broadly at relationships and how they can be expressed. For example, primary students can explore simple functions such as the number of cupcakes needed for different numbers of children attending a party. Functions at this level can be understood concretely, without using symbols.

More complex functions are relationships between two or more things and can often be expressed as a formula. For example, in geometry, there is a functional relationship between the area of a rectangle and its length and width (area = l x w). Temperature conversion formulas involving Fahrenheit and Celsius, such as: $F° = (C° \times 1.8) + 32$, provide another example of a function. Many functions can be expressed algebraically and this connects us to the other aspect of this rainbow arc…

Algebra:

Algebra has been defined as the language of mathematics, or as generalized arithmetic. It's a way of making the specific universal. Algebra uses variables, operations, and symbolic representation. Algebra plays an important role when we want to express the relationship among quantities in a general form. So functions and algebra can't help but be integrated with one another!

Many of us may remember algebra from our high school years. Often we were taught what to do to solve problems without much understanding of the reasons behind what we were doing. In today's classrooms, primary students can begin by exploring algebra informally with concrete materials. For example, students can use bear counters to find out the answer to this question—if there are five bears in the container and they need a total of seven bears to be there—how many more bears should they add? This kind of missing addend problem and simple function problems help lay the foundation for later work and the development of algebraic thinking.

To further develop their abilities, students need opportunities to represent number patterns with tables and graphs and to verbalize their rules and create equations for them. As students explore areas of the curriculum that can be connected to algebra, we need to take advantage of teachable moments. For example, many geometric relationships can be expressed algebraically and generalized using variables. For example, the volume of a sphere is $V = 4/3\ \pi r^3$. We want students to understand algebra so they can add the powerful tools of algebra—variables, symbols, operations, and equations—to their mathematics backpack.

All of these strands are meant to be part of mathematics programs for all students, at all grade levels. Of course, the ways they are represented in the curriculum differ depending on grade level and experience. In the early years, a foundation is laid on which to build deeper understandings and skills in later grades.

Two new and innovative GEMS guides on algebra are now under development. The first is entitled *Algebraic Reasoning for Grades 3-5* and the second is *Adventures in Algebra for Grades 1-2.* Both are scheduled to become available during 2003. Check with GEMS for more information.

In the Tower of Hanoi problem from the GEMS guide Math Around the World, students generate a T-table, create a graph, and write an algebraic equation to arrive at a solution:

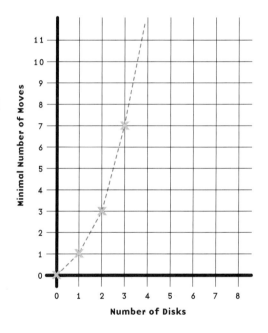

# of Disks	Minimal # of Moves
1	1
2	3
3	7
.	.
.	.
.	.
x	2^x-1

Graph of the Minimal Number of Moves to solve the Tower of Hanoi puzzle depending upon the # of disks used.

"Part of being able to compute fluently means making smart choices about which tools to use when."
NCTM, *Principles and Standards for School Mathematics,* page 35.

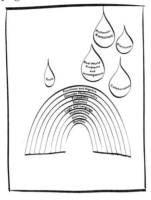

"Representing numbers with various physical materials should be a major part of mathematics instruction in the elementary grades."
NCTM, *Principles and Standards for School Mathematics,* page 33.

"The teacher's role in choosing worthwhile problems and mathematical tasks is crucial."
NCTM, *Principles and Standards for School Mathematics,* page 53.

Raindrops: Tools and Strategies

Next we are going to add some important elements to our rainbow—the raindrops that act as prisms to separate light that goes through them into colors. In this metaphor, the raindrops represent the tools and strategies for making mathematics come alive in the classroom.

The first raindrop is **TOOLS**
Put the "Tools" raindrop on the felt board (or add the "Raindrops" overhead)

Mathematical tools include the concrete materials, such as pattern blocks, dice, cubes, as well as calculators and computers. Students need to have access to a wide range of tools and, over time, learn how to choose the best one to help solve a problem. Since we live in a technological world, students need to gain skills and experience using technological tools to be prepared to enter the work force. The classroom environment also needs to support student learning. No longer is the teacher the sole dispenser of information and knowledge.

This next raindrop is…**DISCOURSE**
Put "Discourse" raindrop on felt board
Discourse is the way knowledge is constructed and exchanged in the classroom. Both the teacher and the students play important roles in shaping the discourse. Teachers need to be skillful facilitators who orchestrate the communication and learning of mathematics by posing questions, guiding discussions, allowing students to grapple with problems, providing content, and so on, as well as being skillful at which intervention (if any) to use and when. The classroom environment needs to support open dialogue and engage all students in mathematical thinking and learning. Through discourse, students are active participants in their own learning, which connects to the next raindrop…

COLLABORATION
Put the "Collaboration" raindrop on the felt board.

Surveys of Fortune 500 companies cite the ability to work cooperatively and to collaborate with others as the single most important quality they look for in future employees. Our classrooms can help develop these abilities by having students work together in teams and groups to solve problems. Collaboration also fosters peer teaching and allows students to share knowledge with one another. Of course, students also need opportunities to work independently.

The *kind* of problems students are asked to solve is also important.

REAL-WORLD PROBLEMS AND INVESTIGATIONS

Put the "Real-World Problems and Investigations" raindrop on the felt board.

Problems that connect with their real-world experiences provide an important entry point to engage students in looking for solutions. Do you remember problems like these?—"Two trains leave from the same station and one travels at 55 mph and the other at 45 mph. If the slower train leaves at 1 p.m., and the faster train leaves at 2:30 p.m, what time will the faster train pass the slower train?" Problems of this type were often given to students without helping them develop understanding of the underlying reasoning and problem-solving method involved, and without connection to the students' real world experiences.

In contrast, the problems we present to our students need to be compelling and have multiple access points—and, in many cases, multiple solutions. Some problems should require rigorous work and lead students to go beyond the classroom walls to find solutions or gain needed information. These are **investigations.** They are done over time and take sustained work to arrive at solutions. An example of an investigation is illustrated by a simple question: How much money does it take to raise a cat? To answer this question many aspects of raising a cat must be investigated, some of which involve mathematics. (You may want to ask what mathematics would be used. Is there one "right" answer to the question?)

Since we are teaching differently and students are working and learning in non-traditional ways, our assessment of student work likewise needs to changed to reflect that. The next raindrop…

AUTHENTIC ASSESSMENT

Put the "Authentic Assessment" raindrop on the felt board.

addresses that change. We need to use assessment techniques that allow students to communicate what they have learned. Classroom discourse provides one window on student understanding. Math journals, projects, portfolios, models, and presentations are some other ways we can assess what students know and what they still need to work on. Our assessment must be in "sync" with our methods of instruction.

The Sun and Its Rays

We put the raindrops up to create prisms that divide light into colors, but we still need a light source to shine through them. Let's add the **SUN** now…
Put the "Sun" on the felt board (or place the Sun and rays on the overhead).

Another example of an investigation would be: The city wants to fence off a piece of property to create a community park. The park will be situated along the river that runs through the city, and the city planners want the park to be as large as possible. The cost and quality of fencing materials varies (a table gives specifics on materials and price) and the project has a budget of $1000 for the fencing costs. You are asked to submit a design for the park that includes the amount of fencing you can purchase (with rationale for the kind of fencing selected), and the shape you think will allow for the largest area possible within the fence. Be sure to include the dimensions of the shape. This kind of investigation is driven by mathematics and requires the use of geometry, measurement, logic, and number sense.

"Assessment should become a routine part of the ongoing classroom activity rather than an interruption."
NCTM, *Principles and Standards for School Mathematics,* page 23.

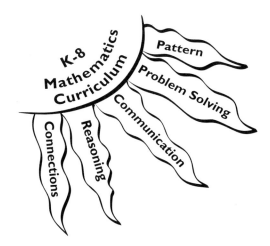

What's next in this pattern?
Students could justify several solutions!

"Conjecture is a major pathway to discovery."
NCTM, *Principles and Standards for School Mathematics*, page 57.

"Reflection and communication are intertwined processes in mathematics education."
NCTM, *Principles and Standards for School Mathematics*, page 61.

The Sun represents the K–8 curriculum. The rays that emanate from it and shine through the raindrops to create the colors of the rainbow are important aspects of all K–8 mathematics programs. These rays represent the process standards of the mathematics curriculum. We need to employ them as we present content with appropriate teaching practices. These rays are:

PATTERNS
Put the "Patterns" ray on the felt board.

Patterns are everywhere—in nature, art, science, music, and history, and they are at the heart of mathematics. Mathematics has even been called the "science of patterns." A pattern can be found in anything that repeats itself over and over. Finding, making, and extending patterns is fundamental to mathematics. Looking for patterns is a powerful problem-solving tool. As the mind searches for patterns, sense can be made from what may at first appear to be discrete, separate, and unrelated things or events. Because of its interconnection with all topic areas in mathematics, the patterns ray touches all parts of the rainbow.

PROBLEM SOLVING
Put the "Problem Solving" ray on the felt board.

We've talked about real-world problems and using problem-solving skills as part of our rainbow metaphor, but problem solving encompasses even more—it is also an overall process that permeates the curriculum. It provides the context in which concepts and skills can be learned. As students solve different types of problems, they learn and develop strategies they can apply when they encounter unfamiliar problems.

Similarly, another important overarching part of the curriculum involves
COMMUNICATION
Put the "Communication" ray on the felt board.

Communication provides a way for students to explain what they have learned, whether they do so verbally or in writing, with concrete materials or with pictures and diagrams. Communicating about mathematics provides an opportunity to further reflect on ideas and to clarify thinking.

The next ray, **REASONING...**
Put the "Reasoning" ray on the felt board.
is closely connected to both problem solving and communication.

Mathematics is reasoning—we cannot do math without it. Students need to gain confidence in their ability to reason and justify their thinking. This ability grows as students have experiences that demonstrate that math makes sense—it is not about memorizing rules and procedures.

"A mathematical proof is a formal way of expressing particular kinds of reasoning and justication."
NCTM, *Principles and Standards for School Mathematics*, page 56..

Students need to be able to see **CONNECTIONS**
Put the "Connections" ray on the felt board.

This refers to connections within mathematics and between mathematics and other subject areas as well as in the real world. **None of the topic areas in the rainbow are meant to be taught in isolation—the metaphor itself is one of colors blending. Similarly, as we approach and seek to solve a problem, many different areas of math come into play.** We also need to build bridges between mathematics and other subject areas—math can be successfully integrated into science, art, social studies, physical education, and other disciplines when we take the time to make those connections. And most importantly, we want students to see that math is not just an academic exercise that occurs only in schools—it an important aspect of the world they live in!

Pots of Gold

Of course, if you pardon a departure from real-world science, rainbows also bring to mind the proverbial **pot of gold** at the end. The song, "Over the Rainbow," says, "…the dreams that we dare to dream really do come true…" and it is literally true that our children's mathematical ability can open doors and help them realize their dreams! Reflecting that, our pots of gold represent:

MATH POWER   **FOR ALL STUDENTS**
Put the pots of gold "Math Power" and "For All Students" on the felt board (or place the last overhead).

The mathematics education programs we implement should develop students' abilities as well as their belief that they have power to do mathematics. They need to be able to approach problems and solve them with confidence. And this power must be made accessible to ALL students. We need to meet the needs of all students regardless of background, gender, language, learning or physical challenges. In creating our curriculum, we need to take these factors into account and be sure that everyone is given ample opportunity to acquire the knowledge and skills they deserve and need.

Conclusion

With this rainbow vision, mathematics can be explored in all its richness and its connection to science, technology, other fields of study, and the real world. Access to mathematics in school is directly connected to obtaining a college education and to employment and career success. **It is a powerful key to the future—one which no child should be denied.**

Through the dedicated work of teachers and educators, with the active involvement of parents, it is our hope that all students will have the opportunity to experience and acquire the vitality, excitement, usefulness, and power of mathematics. In this way, the rainbow of mathematics will be transformed from vision to reality.

"The opportunity for students to experience mathematics in a context is important."
NCTM, *Principles and Standards for School Mathematics,* page 66.

"Mathematics can and must be learned by all students."
NCTM, *Principles and Standards for School Mathematics,* page 13.

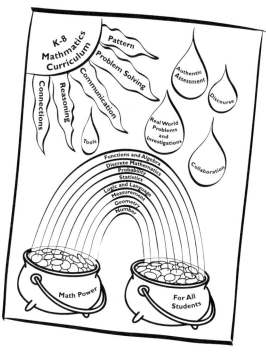

"The vision of equity in mathematics education challenges a pervasive societal belief in North America that only some students are capable of learning mathematics."
NCTM, *Principles and Standards for School Mathematics,* page 12.

Another Rainbow Vision

We said in the introduction to this handbook that each presenter would need to tailor the presentation for the audience. In many cases, such adjustments would concern how deeply to delve into the mathematics, or focusing on parental concerns, etc. Many presenters may want to modify categories to more tation can be closely correspond t ttoe NCTM Prin*ciples and Standards* or state frameworks.

One of the reviewers of this handbook, Steve Rakow, 1998-99 President of the National Science Teacher's Association (NSTA), in addition to raising the need to highlight *Standards 2000*, also had a more radical and intriguing suggestion for the rainbow metaphor. He commented, "A rainbow is the physical manifestation of light energy being separated into its component parts by water. The light is the input. The rainbow is the outcome."

With this in mind, his vision of the rainbow of mathematics would see the Sun as representing the entire domain of mathematics. The Sun's rays would then be the "subject areas" (which we have called strands)—number, algebra, geometry, etc. The rain drops would be the tools and strategies that allow students to make use of these "subject areas." In Rakow's version of the metaphor, the rainbow is what the students derive as a result of their learning—**mathematical power.** (In his version there would also be no need for the pots of gold at the end of the rainbow, about which he expressed the concern that such treasures are of course in the realm of mythology, not science!)

And while we're on the subject of science, we might add that nearly every drawing of rain drops falling depicts them as having a sharp upper point—that has become the recognized symbol. Scientifically speaking, however, small rain drops are nearly spherical. Larger raindrops are distorted by the pressure of the moving air, but, rather than being pointed, this makes them somewhat flattened. Surface tension of the water acts like a stretched "bag" around the water and, unless some other force is acting on it, pulls it into a spherical shape.

From the GEMS Network News: *It is with great sadness that we must record the tragic death, on June 9, 2001 of Dr. Steven J. Rakow, educator extraordinaire, at the age of 48, after a long and courageous battle following a bicycling accident. Steve was well-known nationwide, having served as President of the NSTA, written many articles, and presented many professional development workshops nationally and internationally. Steve was a GEMS Associate and longtime friend of GEMS who advised us on many publications—including this one.*

Music and Mathematics

At several GEMS professional development workshops and institutes, a new, lively element has been added to the "Rainbow of Mathematics" presentation. Here's how it works:

After each of the rainbow strands has been introduced, one of the tables of participants is assigned a sound, rhythm, or makeshift musical instrument to symbolize that strand. That table then practices their sound. You can decide on your own instruments and activities—the following are just examples. For the number strand, all participants at that table count out loud: "1-2-3-4" for a half-minute or so. For geometry, a few metal triangles are provided (or they can be pretend and the participants say "ding" as they strike their imaginary triangles). For measurement a makeshift percussion instrument is played, for example, by rubbing a pencil over the ridges on a plastic ruler. Logic and language can be assigned a slightly complex hand clapping pattern that repeats itself ((1-2-123, 1-2-123) A few small containers to shake dice suffice for the strand of both Statistics and Probability. For Discrete Mathematics, which also involves combinations, participants are given a few toy xylophones and are assigned to play the same four notes in different sequences. For Functions and Algebra, participants can act out a Rube Goldberg-type "function machine," with the last person in the line singing out a note or making a noise of some kind.

When all the rainbow strands have been introduced and explained, and each sound practiced, then all the sounds can be put together at the end, with the presenter serving as conductor, and the whole room taking part in the musical activity. The underlying point then becomes musically manifest— all the strands of the rainbow mathematics work and weave together. A teacher is a facilitator, an orchestra conductor, providing ways for students to work together to achieve mathematical power. ∎

In this section of the handbook, we take a look at the strong currents of mathematics that run throughout the GEMS series, beginning with guides for early childhood, (Pre/K–1), followed by a detailed discussion of the GEMS K–5 mathematics guides, and ending with a summary of guides for older students and strong emphasis on mathematics in many of the GEMS science guides for upper elementary and middle school students.

Early Childhood Means Early Math Experiences

Study after study emphasizes the importance of reaching preschool and early childhood students with high-quality age-appropriate educational experiences, especially in math and science. GEMS units for young children lend themselves to meaningful **integration of math and science** along with language, literature, art, music, and drama. These activities that tap into children's interest and curiosity in the natural world provide a wonderful way to develop mathematical concepts within the context of the whole curriculum.

Starting at the preschool level and in kindergarten, we want to develop children's **logical thinking skills,** and one of the first steps toward that goal is learning how to sort and classify objects. In the *Tree Homes* unit, children bring in toy bears that they **sort and classify** in many ways. In the *Eggs Eggs Everywhere* unit, children open toy eggs and discover lizards, birds, bugs, and other animals they sort and classify. The animals children create in *Animal Defenses* also lend themselves to sorting and classifying and are of high interest to the children since they designed them!

The three units on insects—*Ant Homes Under the Ground, Buzzing A Hive,* and *Ladybugs*—provide opportunities to make models of insects which develop **number sense** as children count out the three body parts, six legs, and two antennae on each. This process prepares them for categorizing animals by their physical structures. As children play a game that simulates penguin behavior in the *Penguins And Their Young* unit, they **add and subtract using concrete materials.** Likewise, by using a model of an ant nest, children use **number skills** to fill the ant hill. The number experiences woven into each guide are always in relevant context so children make meaningful connections of numbers to the real world and their own experiences.

Similarly, children explore **geometry** informally by doing such things as watching frozen **three-dimensional geometric shapes** melt in a tub of water (*Penguins And Their Young*), and discovering what objects will roll down a ramp (*Eggs Eggs Everywhere*). In making the cardboard tree model, children use boxes and cut ellipses in them for the tree holes (*Tree Homes*). While making ladybugs, children explore **symmetry** both in ladybugs and also through related activities. As children investigate bee hives, they learn about hexagons. In all the units, there are opportunities to explore **shapes** and **spatial relationships.**

Young children are very interested in themselves and in each other and often make comparisons. Such comparisons can be a springboard to understanding **measurement.** Comparative measurement is also emphasized in *Penguins And Their Young,* as children compare their height with that of a life-size poster of an emperor penguin. They also compare their hands and feet with the size of the emperor's egg and chick. In *Tree Homes,* the model tree's holes are also a measurement tool and are used to determine animals that can fit within each. In *Mother Opossum and Her Babies,* children explore **non-standard units** as they measure mother opossum and use their models of young opossums to measure familiar objects. Children count their pockets and have an opportunity to count by 1s, 5s, and 10s. In *Elephants and Their Young*, children have opportunities to explore volume and weight, and use non-standard units to fill the area of an elephant's footprint and their own.

It may seem that very young children are not ready to grapple with **statistics,** but we can provide experiences that allow them to **organize data and make sense out of it.** After sorting in the *Eggs Eggs Everywhere* unit, students move on to graphing the animals and making number statements about the data organized on a bar graph. **Graphing** is a key component to organizing data from hands-on experiments in the *Sifting Through Science* unit. In *Ant Homes Under the Ground,* children collect data informally as they visit ant homes in the outdoor environment and their classroom over time. In *Terrarium Habitats,* children observe and record data about what is happening over time.

As we have said, **pattern** is an underlying theme in all of mathematics. Through studying **life cycles** of animals, children can observe patterns in the natural world. Children make a life cycle book as part of the ladybug unit to concretely illustrate the life cycle. In *Buzzing A Hive,* a series of bee posters show the bee's development from egg to adult. Children also **enact patterns** when they simulate bees doing a bee dance.

These highlighted mathematics activities are just some of the many ways that mathematics is integrated into each unit. "Going Further" suggestions are also provided to deepen or extend this learning. Teachers often add their own activities and include ideas from other programs. By making math meaningful and teaching it in context, a strong foundation of concepts and skills is provided for further development in later grades. These GEMS guides can help you build that foundation: *Animal Defenses; Ant Homes Under the Ground; Buzzing A Hive; Eggs Eggs Everywhere; Elephants and Their Young; Hide A Butterfly; Ladybugs; Mother Opossum and Her Babies; Penguins And Their Young; Sifting Through Science; Terrarium Habitats;* and *Tree Homes.*

The GEMS K–5 Mathematics Program

There are a growing number of GEMS guides that have mathematics at their heart. In particular, at the early- to mid-elementary level, *Build It! Festival, Frog Math, Treasure Boxes, Group Solutions, Group Solutions, Too!, Math on the Menu,* and *In All Probability*—and two coming on algebra—blend together to provide compelling experiences in mathematics across the math strands. As they introduce students to pivotal math concepts, these guides also provide opportunities to build and practice important skills and abilities. The guides truly represent the rainbow of mathematics spectrum—exploring the major content strands in age-appropriate ways and reflecting the best teaching practices. They are designed for all students, fully embodying collaborative learning, and make mathematics relevant to student's lives and to the real world.

Coherent mathematical threads are woven within each unit and interweave throughout the entire GEMS K–5 mathematics program. Skills and concepts are introduced and developed with many opportunities to apply them. In *Frog Math,* the first session **introduces attributes** and has students focus on attributes through use of games. Building upon this, in Session 2 students use **attributes to sort and classify,** and then are challenged to create their own unique sorts, as well as determine how classmates sorted. Going deeper in Session 3, students organize their hand-crafted buttons by **attributes on a graph and make interpretations**

about that graph. Student are thus developing many skills—including **observation, comparing, number, sorting and classifying, organization, and logical thinking and reasoning**—as they acquire conceptual understanding about logic and statistics. This thread is picked up in *Treasure Boxes* as students again sort, classify, and graph treasure items. Students apply their knowledge of **sorting and classifying using treasures** and go further with the introduction of a new tool—a **Venn diagram.** In addition, **graphing** is taken a step further as students record their graphs and make **true statements** about them. Again, graphing is revisited and further developed throughout *In All Probability* and is a vital tool for understanding **probability and statistics.** In *Group Solutions, Too!* graph-reading is cleverly integrated into a number of the **cooperative logic challenges.** Furthermore, in both *Group Solutions* and *Group Solutions, Too!,* there are two families of activities that have students **focus on attributes to solve problems.** In this way, these units weave together experiences for students to gain conceptual understanding about sorting and classifying as well as organizing data in a variety of ways. In addition, this mathematical understanding is developed over time and in different contexts that are meaningful to young students.

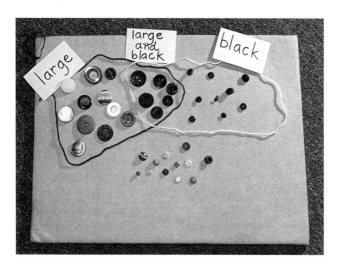

The GEMS K–5 mathematics guides are firmly in alignment with recommendations of leading mathematics educators, such as the NCTM's standards for school mathematics for K–5 programs, and many state and district frameworks. A detailed listing of how each of the GEMS K–5 mathematics guides support the NCTM Standards can be found as Appendix C of this handbook on page 39. As can be seen from that compilation, a flexible and integrated reflection of these

standards is intrinsic to the GEMS K–4 mathematics units. Among the standards strongly exemplified are the first four: problem solving, reasoning, communication, and making connections to other areas of mathematics and other subject areas. Among major standards-based content areas interwoven in these GEMS guides are: number sense and numeration; geometry and spatial sense; discrete mathematics; and statistics and probability.

Underlying the NCTM Standards and other leading recommendations are stated assumptions that the math curriculum should: be conceptually oriented; actively involve children in doing mathematics; emphasize the development of children's mathematical thinking and reasoning abilities; emphasize the application of mathematics; include a broad range of content; and make appropriate and ongoing use of calculators and computers. The GEMS K–5 mathematics units embody these elements. They are designed to develop mathematical understanding through a conceptual approach. In each unit, students are active participants in their learning; they explore, develop, test, discuss, and apply ideas using physical materials to foster understanding of abstract ideas. This active involvement is also key to the assessments in each unit. During instruction and assessment, discourse is used to promote student thinking and discussion. Students problem solve, then explain and justify the thinking behind the solutions, which further develops critical thinking skills. In addition, there are many opportunities to apply what has been learned. Calculators are used in context, and both *Frog Math* and *Treasure Boxes* have suggested computer activities that connect the on-line learning with the hands-on content-rich activities.

The GEMS K–5 mathematics program uses many approaches to draw students into learning important mathematical concepts. There is effective use of **real-world connections** so all students have interest in and access to the content. For example, buttons and treasure items come from the students' world. These high-interest, inexpensive materials are used to sort, classify, graph, count, divide, play games, and more. The Dowel Design activity in *Build It! Festival* uses newspaper to create dowels for building two- or three-dimensional shapes. Students use pennies, dice, and spinners for statistics and probability activities in *In All Probability* and they are encouraged to make connections between the activities they do in class and related games at home. Students from all backgrounds have

experience with games. In *Frog Math* and *Treasure Boxes,* mathematical content is drawn from exciting games (Button Up, Button Factory, Guess My Sort, Frog Pond, Hop to the Pond, and Treasure Map) that students enjoy playing. In *Math on the Menu,* the real-world context of a Mexican restaurant provides a great "entree" to student investigations in combinatorics, a branch of discrete mathematics. In all the units, students use their creativity in many ways, such as making paper buttons for a graphing activity in *Frog Math,* developing a new version of the Treasure Map game in *Treasure Boxes,* designing their own game sticks in *In All Probability,* creating tessellations in *Build It! Festival,* devising their own cooperative logic games in both volumes of *Group Solutions,* and coming up with diverse menus and flexible table arrangements for a new restaurant in *Math on the Menu.*

Throughout the GEMS K–5 mathematics units, the math content is enriched by developing understandings represented by more than one standard. For example, when playing the games Horse Race in *In All Probability,* or Hop to the Pond in *Frog Math* students generate data to understand the probability behind the game. Students also make predictions, use number sense and whole number operations, gather and interpret data, problem solve and communicate their findings. They thus have experience with many different and yet connected aspects of mathematics. Students are developing their understanding of both content and process aspects, including: statistics and probability, estimation, number sense and numeration, whole number operations, problem solving, communication, reasoning, and making connections. All of the K–5 GEMS math units maintain this level of interconnectedness while developing particular content standards in depth. In addition, many

of the GEMS science guides for early- and mid-elementary grades make excellent complements to the K–5 mathematics guides and have strong mathematical components themselves such as *Sifting Through Science, Bubble Festival, Investigating Artifacts,* and *Secret Formulas.*

Upper Elementary and Middle School

In All Probability, also included above, was designed and tested for Grades 3–6 and has been used quite successfully in 6th grade and above. For those students with prior experience in probability, the activities re-emphasize some important fundamentals then go on to challenge students with some quite **complex probabilities** raised by Native American game sticks, the concluding activity in the guide. Older students will also be more able to relate to issues raised in *In All Probability* concerning how **statistics** can be used and misused in advertising, and in general will bring more **complex thinking and problem-solving skills** to the activities. This guide is particularly strong in providing a series of concrete experiences that, when taken together, develop solid and appropriately sophisticated student understanding—the experiences are designed to enable all students to construct that understanding and to retain and apply basic probability principles.

The *QUADICE* unit features an original game for Grades 4–8 which: provides students with lots of practice in **mental arithmetic, basic operations,** and **strategic thinking;** helps them handle **fractions** with greater confidence; and also explores **probability.** Within the challenging game context, students have the chance to refine **skills in addition, subtraction, division, and multiplication.** A cooperative version of the game is featured to further emphasize **problem-solving strategies** and **cooperative learning.** In Session 4, "How Many Ways," students discover whether or not they can improve their scores by **analyzing the probability that any particular combination of numbers will appear.** This can be introduced simply for students without prior experience with probability, or at a more advanced level for more experienced students. The final session, "QUADICE Puzzles" stimulates students to think about how they would solve particular game situations. The puzzles lead to a better understanding of **constant sum,** constant difference, and constant ratio. In general, *QUADICE* provides plenty of practice in mental arithmetic and strategic thinking. As your students advance through the cooperative game and later challenges, more complicated game strategies and more sophisticated mathematical concepts are explored—all within the fun and challenging framework of a game.

Math Around the World is filled with games and other compelling challenges that bring the **international, multicultural nature of mathematics** to the fore while opening up a rainbow of contentful math learning. As the guide's introduction states, "These activities are replete with mathematics for the middle grades." Some of the mathematics content jumps out clearly—as when students discuss **options and strategies,** discover **numerical and visual patterns,** refine **number sense,** use **mental math,** explore **geometric properties,** and **create, test, and apply theories.**

At other times the underlying mathematics may be less evident, suggesting the need for the teacher to encourage more guided exploration, thought, and investigation. While students enjoy playing Kalah for hours, developing strategies to win, asking them questions after they've played a few games can focus attention on the mathematics—"Is it better to have more beans on your side or on your opponent's side?" "Does it matter who goes first?" The guide includes numerous suggestions for helping guide students through these rich mathematical experiences. Student learning will of course also depend on age and experience— younger students might gain an intuitive understanding of **exponential growth** from The Tower of Hanoi, while older students might extend this understanding to a more formal level, by **deriving the formula for the function** embedded in the puzzle.

The following table and note, (on page xx) adapted from the introduction to *Math Around the World,* provide a sense of the many strands of mathematics woven into the unit. The guide also includes numerous presentation approaches and options, connections to world cultures, geography, history, the social sciences, and literature, and suggests diverse ways for teachers to fit *Math Around the World* into their curriculum.

Science Guides Filled with Math

Starting with some of the earliest and still most popular GEMS guides, math has been embedded in the science that students explore. In the *Bubble-ology* unit, students have opportunities to explore **geometry, measurement, statistics, and function** all within the context of an engaging medium—the bubble! The geometry of bubbles presents itself as students make individual bubbles and then observe their structures in relationship to one another. As they conduct an experiment to determine which bubble solution creates the largest bubble, they take **diameter measurements** of many bubbles, thus collecting data and analyzing it using the **mean (average)** for each solution. Further exploration of bubble solution has students investigate the relationship between the amount of glycerin in the solution and the size of the bubble. This **function is graphed** to determine the optimum amount for making large bubbles. Students also **look for color patterns** to help them predict when a bubble will pop. The grand finale challenges students to apply all that they have learned and to use their critical thinking skills to make a longest lasting bubble. An extensive background section includes some very interesting geometrical and other mathematical information, from the 120° angles in bubble sheets and the **hexagons** in bubble walls to the more complex **polyhedrons** in bubble stacking and issues in **topology.** Clearly, the mathematics and science learning in this unit bubble up together!

Another highly successful and favorite guide—*Investigating Artifacts*—goes well beyond math and science integration to include social studies, language arts, and art. This guide has at its core indigenous and world cultures that are studied through the lens of science and math. The mathematics comes into play when students **sort and classify** natural items from their environment using **Venn diagrams.** From these found objects, masks are crafted which can again be sorted and classified. In addition, students use the masks as simulated **evidence** of a culture and **make inferences** about the peoples who made them. When students make myths about scientific phenomena, they **look for patterns** to explain such events as the phases of the moon or the life cycle of a butterfly. Students collect and record data on maps and charts as they uncover a midden. Again, they make inferences about an unknown culture that left these artifacts behind. Sorting and classifying and further refining classification is of

A look at the games included in the guide and their correlation with GEMS Math Strands

	Logic and Language	Pattern	Number	Algebra	Discrete Mathematics	Functions	Statistics and Probability	Geometry
NIM	★	■	★		■			
Kalah	■	■	■		■			
Tower of Hanoi	■	■	■	★	■	★		
Shongo Networks	■	★	■		★			■
Magic Squares	■	■	★	★				
Game Sticks	■	■	■		★		★	
Games of Alignment	■	■			■			
Hex	★	■			■			■

Please note: It is important to understand that these mathematics strands interweave with each other to create the fabric of mathematical content. Using this metaphor, there are some strands that are more "weft" and others more "warp." For example, in all of these games, the warp is represented by the Pattern and Logic and Language strands. Pattern, seen as the underlying theme that runs through all mathematics, is employed in the games as a tool to develop winning strategies or solve the challenges. The Logic and Language strand also plays a crucial role, as students express their thinking and use diverse problem-solving skills to develop, refine, and communicate strategies. In some of the games these two strands are the most important. In addition, for most of these games there are also strong teaching opportunities to introduce or deepen learning in at least one other strand. To assist you in pinpointing these opportunities, we have used a star (★) to designate those strands which play a vital role in each game and thus provide a strong teaching opportunity. We show a box (■) for strands that are represented in the game, or needed for foundation of understanding, but are not central. For example, in Game Sticks, the Logic and Language and Pattern strands both have boxes to indicate that those strands play a role in the game, but the key areas of mathematics content for this game are found in the Statistics and Probability and Discrete Mathematics strands. For this game, you'll note that the Number strand also has a box. Number sense and the use of computation in context are necessary to express and explain the Discrete Mathematics and Statistics and Probability strands. In this case, Number is not a key area, but part of the warp needed to create a foundation through which the weft can be woven. You need not focus on the strands that are starred—the games are rich in content and learning through the Pattern and Logic and Language strands, and Number also runs through most of the games. In and of themselves, the games provide many other exciting learning opportunities. We are aware that the Measurement strand is missing from this chart. That is because none of these games have a strong connection to that mathematical strand. This emphasizes a final and important point—it is not at all necessary (nor do we intend) for any one game or any one mathematics activity to encompass all the strands. While it is true that many activities and games interweave several related strands, it is also true that less can be more, and making a more focused connection to fewer strands can mean making a stronger connection.

course a central component of both math and science, and is featured in many GEMS mathematics units. In addition, sorting and classification is a key element of *Liquid Explorations, Sifting Through Science, Stories in Stone,* and many other guides.

Secret Formulas represents a very effective early elementary integration of science and mathematics. The experience students gain with **measurement** centers on **non-standard units** of measure such as spoons, straw droppers, and toothpicks. This is a great way to prepare students for using standard units. **Comparison** is also woven through the activities, as students compare amounts and **attributes** of ingredients and their effects. **Numbers are also used in context** throughout the unit, as students determine, for example, the number of spoonfuls of corn starch needed to make their ideal paste, or drops of vanilla for their own special cola. From the science point of view, the guide's strong emphasis on cause and effect as a precursor for later experimentation also suggests a foundational experience for the mathematical idea of **function**—there is a functional relationship between the amount of sugar added and the sweetness of the cola; similar relationships exist between the amount of an ingredient and the attributes of toothpaste or ice cream. Of course, any activities that relate to cooking, food preparation, and many chemistry procedures—for example, mixing of different ingredients in a chemical reaction—of necessity involve number and measurement of many kinds.

You don't need a magnifying glass to find the math in GEMS mystery guides. As students take on the role of detectives, they put their **logical thinking and problem-solving skills** to the test—from **looking for patterns** to using **deductive reasoning.** What they piece together is the information that is often gathered from forensic tests. Much of forensic science involves **collecting, organizing, and interpreting data.** For example, in the *Fingerprinting* unit, students begin by **sorting and classifying** a set of fingerprints, and from these explorations, they learn a classification system. To solve a fictitious crime they apply this system. Chromatograms are a key to solving a mystery in *Crime Lab Chemistry.* Part of cracking these cases is based on the ability to **make inferences based on the evidence.** In the *Mystery Festival* guide, students visit a "crime scene," conduct many forensic tests, and **make comparisons,** all in order to determine whodunit. Not only are these forensic units of high interest to stu-

dents, they pose a **problem to solve within a real-world context.** The Hexacarbon Mystery in *Learning About Learning* provides another example of how the mystery format motivates and deepens logical thinking skills. And *Environmental Detectives* presents a complex environmental mystery.

Global Warming & the Greenhouse Effect is another well-known GEMS unit that integrates a great deal of mathematics by the very nature of its subject. Its main question—whether or not increased production of carbon dioxide due to human industrial and technological activity is causing an increase in world temperature—depends on mathematical analysis. **Measurement of many kinds**—from estimated world temperature derived from analysis of polar ice layers to gauging the levels which the ocean may rise as temperatures increase—is essential to this unit. Throughout the unit, students evaluate **complex graphs.** They play a game that builds in the **statistical probability** involved in whether or not the Earth's atmosphere retains or deflects photons that can result in an increase of CO_2. A similar **pattern** or **variation** results in the greenhouse effect. Students compare the **relative concentration** of carbon dioxide in air, human breath, car exhaust, and the chemical reaction of baking soda and vinegar. In effect, the entire issue of global warming also reflects the mathematical strand referred to as **function**—the theory supposes that an increase in the amount of CO_2 in the atmosphere will lead to a proportional increase in world temperature, which will in turn lead to a rise in sea level, with impact on agriculture and many other consequences. **Independent thinking** and **problem solving,** so important in both math and science, are powerfully addressed in this unit, which allows students to make up their own minds, based on **complex sets of evidence and data,** about the environmental issue of global warming.

Another substantial environmental GEMS unit, *Acid Rain,* is grounded in mathematics. In order for students to understand what makes rain acidic, they need to comprehend the **logarithmic nature** of the acid-neutral-base continuum (2 on the pH scale is 10 times more acidic than 3). This is also a crucial part of the GEMS guide *Of Cabbages and Chemistry.* Also in *Acid Rain,* students conduct an experiment on the effect of different **concentrations** of a common acid (vinegar) on plant growth. The Startling Statements game in Session 3 acquaints students with considerable **statistical information** on acid rain, often presented in varying **percentages.**

The GEMS guide *Discovering Density* builds from a series of compelling hands-on experiences to bring students to a more abstract understanding of density, including the **mathematical formula for density,** which is expressed in **algebraic** fashion. Students work with and **apply the formula** as, based on their calculations, they **predict** how liquids of different density will layer, then test their predictions.

Geometry and other aspects of spatial visualization are significant components of a number of GEMS science guides. Examples in *Bubble-ology* were mentioned earlier. In Session 3 of *Stories in Stone,* "The Shapes of Mineral Crystals," students create paper models of characteristic crystal shapes—**cube, hexagonal prism,** and **pyramid**—then can go on to create **tetrahedrons, octahedrons, dodecahedrons,** and **pyritohedrons.** The guide includes **sorting and classification** activities, as well as an experiment modeling the formation of crystals, involving comparison of crystal formation at different temperatures. The mathematics even extends to the odes of Chilean poet Pablo Neruda, interspersed throughout the guide. The poem near the crystal shapes activity refers to the crystalline shapes of Earth's minerals as "a whole buried geometry."

Another kind of **spatial visualization** figures into the **maze** activity in *Learning About Learning.* Students reflect on their learning and teaching abilities within this context. The pathway of a maze resonates with the mathematical ideas of **networks** raised in the "Shongo Networks" portion of *Math Around the World.* Later in *Learning About Learning* students simulate experiments on the number and growth of dendrites in nerve cells of the human brain, using a **counting** and **statistical sampling** approach that experimenters used to **estimate** the effect of impoverished or enriched environments on the growth of brain cells.

Speaking of sampling, mathematical ideas connected with biological **sampling** techniques, as well as **tracking** and **mapping** activities, are well represented in GEMS biology guides such as *Animals in Action, Mapping Animal Movements, Mapping Fish Habitats,* and *Schoolyard Ecology.*

In addition to the many science guides already mentioned that involve **measurement** and **number,** the GEMS *Earthworms* guide centers on **counting and recording** the number of pulses in the circulation system of an earthworm at different temperatures. From these measurements emerges a **function** that defines the term poikilothermic—the pulse rate of the earthworm depends on temperature—the colder the temperature, the slower the pulse rate. In *Hot Water and Warm Homes from Sunlight,* students build model houses and determine the effects of size, color, and number of windows on the amount of heat produced from sunlight. With each experiment, they **measure** temperature and **graph** results.

In *Paper Towel Testing* students "soak up" a great deal of mathematics, including **measurement** and learning about **money in a real-world context.** The tests involve issues of absorbency and wet strength and students come up with their own ways to **measure** and **rate** these attributes. The guide takes on more real-life and mathematics connections as students seek to determine which brand is the "best buy" by assessing the attributes in light of **cost per unit** of paper towel. In *Vitamin C Testing,* another consumer science unit, students test for then **graph** the **proportion** of Vitamin C in a variety of drinks.

Several GEMS guides invite students to explore the realm of **large numbers, distance, scale,** and the **scale modeling** of vast distances or geologic time spans. *Microscopic Explorations* provides students with a wide range of experiences with "the world of the small" and practice with a scientific instrument that greatly enhances the power of the human eye. The newly revised *River Cutters* devotes a session to fostering student understanding of the **"deep time"** over which geologic formations take place, as well as comparing river formation over time with human history. In both *Moons of Jupiter* and *Messages from Space,* students use proportional reasoning to create **scale models** of the solar system and **relative sizes** of planets. Students gain a sense of the **enormous distances** between bodies in space. In *Messages from Space,* students consider the **probability** of the existence of life in other star systems. They learn that while many scientists believe that there is a distinct possibility that life exists elsewhere, it is important to recognize that the **vast distances** involved in space travel also cast extreme doubt on the sensationalized reports of "alien" visitors from outer space!

Some guides dovetail with each other to combine the mathematics and science content. That is certainly the case with the guides, *Experimenting with Model Rockets* and *Height-O-Meters.* In *Experimenting with Model Rockets,* students build model rockets as the vehicle to explore the concept of controlled experimentation. A key part of the experimentation process involves determining the **altitude (linear height)** of the launched rockets. To have the skills to do this, students first explore the concept of triangulation as it is developed in the *Height-O-Meters* guide. To begin, they **construct and calibrate** their own **measurement tools** called "height-o-meters" which are more commonly known as clinometers. As students use their height-o-meters, they learn how to **measure angles and distances** and determine heights based on the **concept of triangulation.** As the class practices using the height-o-meter, there are opportunities to use **estimation skills,** work in the **metric system, gather data, calculate averages,** and **record data**—all of which prepares them to apply their understanding of **triangulation** to the rocketry experiment.

Variables play a large role both in science and mathematics. In mathematics, one way that variables are used is to express functions algebraically. These **functions are graphed** with the independent variable represented on the x-axis and the dependent variable on the y-axis. In science, variables appear in the context of experimentation. The control variables stay constant throughout experimentation. The independent variables are those that may affect the results, but do not influence one another directly. The dependent variables are observed outcomes and are influenced by any of the independent variables. Scientists set up experiments with variables, and then **make observations and collect data** over time. To **analyze the outcomes** of the experiments, the results are often **graphed just as the variables in algebraic functions.** This link between mathematics and science is one that exemplifies the role mathematics has in scientific investigation. Many GEMS guides, including *Hot Water and Warm Homes from Sunlight, Paper Towel Testing, Vitamin C Testing,* and *Experimenting with Model Rockets* have variables at their core. The experiments necessitate data collection and analysis, often using graphing and/or statistics to interpret results. ∎

GEMS mathematics and integrated math/science GEMS units are strongly supportive of leading national standards in mathematics, including the recommendations of the National Council of Teachers of Mathematics (NCTM).

In mathematics, science, and life, nothing ever stands still—and, as noted earlier, even as this handbook is written, significant new NCTM standards and principles are evolving for the new century. Later presentations of The Rainbow of Mathematics *will no doubt reflect many of these changes. See Appendices C and D for more on the NCTM Standards.*

These standards, the major mathematics strands described by the rainbow metaphor, and the other key elements of excellent mathematics instruction, need to be seen holistically. Like the colors of the rainbow, they are interwoven and blend with each other. How such strands and exemplary practices are applied, of course, depends on each unique situation. Early experiences lay the foundation for more complex and sophisticated understandings in later grades. Inquiry-driven activities that make strong connections to the experience and real lives of students are particularly effective and successful in conveying major concepts in memorable ways. Units that exemplify the integration of math and science deepen student understanding of both subjects, their strong connection to each other, and their daily application in real-world careers.

It is very important for teachers, educators, parents, administrators, policymakers, and community leaders to be aware of modern approaches to mathematics (and science) education. In recent years, the move toward national standards, which was spurred in great part in its initial stages by mathematics educators, has established positive criteria and goals for student learning. It is hoped that this handbook and especially the presentation of "The Rainbow of Mathematics" will foster improved understanding and thus contribute to educational change.

By interweaving your own combinations of mathematics strands and exemplary pedagogical approaches in the classroom activities you present, you will be fostering the growth of mathematical power in your students. In turn, students will gain knowledge, skills, and a solid sense of confidence, and will be better prepared for the challenges of more advanced mathematics in high school and beyond. Student acquisition of mathematical power can be the key to opening opportunities for higher education and fulfilling career options.

Exciting activities, like those found in the GEMS program and in other excellent math and science programs, can help you reach all students by providing a variety of learning modes suited for differing learning styles. The wonderful multiplicity of *Math Around the World* is worth a thousand words about the brilliant contributions of world cultures to mathematics. Both volumes of *Group Solutions* (as well as almost every other GEMS math or science guide) foster cooperative learning and collaborative problem solving, thereby preparing students for the real world of work while helping bridge and respect differences of culture and background. And, as we have seen with our own eyes, again and again, in school after school, the entire class, including hard-to-reach or highly distracted students, is drawn into the hands-on activities and active learning intrinsic to all GEMS units.

There are many other examples to demonstrate that GEMS units, in addition to providing key science and math content, also keep in mind the big ideas and larger goals—GEMS guides "keep their eyes on the prize." It is our hope that this handbook, as well as other GEMS handbooks and the growing variety of GEMS teacher's guides, will assist you in helping your students reach that prize of educational success— symbolized by the twin pots of gold at the end of the rainbow of mathematics. Their treasure shines like the light of learning in the inquiring minds of students everywhere. ■

APPENDICES

Appendix A:

Mathematics Strands Further Defined

Appendix B:

Table—Math Strands in GEMS Guides

Appendix C:

GEMS K–5 Math Guides and NCTM Standards

Appendix D:

More on the NCTM Standards

Appendix E:

Bibliography and Web Links

Math Rainbow Presentation Tips and Summary Outline

Overhead Masters for Math Rainbow Presentation

Appendix A:
Mathematics Strands Further Defined

"The Rainbow of Mathematics" presentation provides an overview of the areas of mathematics needed for creating excellent school programs. To delve more deeply into each of the topic areas—or content strands—represented in the rainbow, we include this appendix. In addition, we include a few notable exemplars from the GEMS series for each content area. These examples are illustrative and by no means exhaustive—there are many other GEMS units that connect to each mathematical content area, as illustrated in the chart on page 39.

NUMBER

The concept of number permeates all of mathematics as well as our daily lives. Numbers are used to define quantities and relationships, to measure, to make comparisons, to interpret information, and to solve problems. As part of developing a foundation in mathematics, there is a need to gain an understanding of numbers—where they come from, how they are used, and how the system of numbers works. Beginning with concrete, real-world experiences, numbers are understood through counting "how many" or measuring "how much." Number sense is developed by representing numbers in different ways, perceiving relationships among numbers, and developing a knowledge of operations.

The counting numbers {1, 2, 3, 4...} are the first numbers young students work with. When we add zero to the set, it grows and becomes the set of whole numbers {0, 1, 2, 3, 4...}. By working with these numbers, an understanding of the relative size of numbers is developed and of number/quantity concepts. As we expand the set of whole number to include negative whole numbers, we have the set of integers {...-3, -2, -1, 0, 1, 2, 3, ...}. Building on this foundation, we can delve into a larger set of numbers— rational numbers. A rational number is a number that can be written in the form of a fraction such that the numerator and the denominator are integers *and* the denominator is not equal to zero. For example, the fraction -4/5 is rational since the numerator and denominator are both integers (-4 and 5) and the denominator (5) is not equal to 0. However, the fraction—square root of 2/5—is not a rational

number, since the square root of 2 is not an integer. The following diagram visually illustrates the relationships among these sets of numbers:

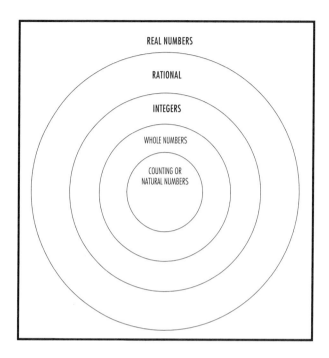

Advanced study of numbers includes an exploration of irrational numbers, real numbers, complex numbers, and unique numbers such as *pi* and the properties of the numbers of 0 and 1.

Often, when we first think of numbers, we connect them to computation—totaling a bill, knowing the multiplication tables, being able to do mental math, etc. Computation is definitely one key part of the number strand. Sometimes it is assumed that, through rote practice and memorization, people acquire the ability to do problems that relate to computation. However, to be successful at computation in the many forms we encounter it, it is also crucial to have an understanding of computation on a conceptual level. That understanding provides the basis for solving problems— simply knowing the multiplication tables through memorization and rote drill is not sufficient. Computation is just one part of the number strand—that needs to be kept in perspective. The concept of number has many other important components, such as estimation, place value, fractions, decimals, percentages, and number theory. Technology also plays a role in developing number sense by providing tools—calculators, computers, and web browsers—to enrich student understanding.

Concepts relating to number and numbers themselves are of course woven into all areas of mathematics, as well as in science and many other disciplines. In geometry, polygons are defined by the number of sides, and the number of degrees in an angle defines and determines its classification. Likewise, in measurement, we use numbers to define the cups in a gallon, the days in a week, and height in inches or centimeters. As we solve problems using logic, the idea of number often helps us to articulate a strategy or find a pattern. In statistics, the data collected can be organized on graphs, tables, and charts that rely on numbers. Probabilities are expressed as fractions, decimals, and percentages, and in discrete mathematics, combinations and permutations are generated using numbers. An understanding of the counting numbers through irrational numbers comes into play to solve a quadratic equation.

The GEMS guide, *Frog Math: Predict, Ponder, Play,* provides many opportunities to use numbers in context. From looking at the number of holes in a button to examining the data on button graphs, students count and connect numbers to quantities. Students also estimate how many frogs are in a jar and use a place value board to count the actual number. Individually, they also estimate and count how many beans they can hold in one handful. While playing the Hop to the Pond games, students practice number recognition as well as the addition facts for the numbers that can be generated by two standard dice. The data analysis of the outcome of the game also uses numbers. And, as would be expected, one way or another, the concept of number plays a part in all GEMS guides.

GEOMETRY

Geometry is the study of two- and three-dimensional shapes. Since all the objects in our world have a shape or form, geometry links mathematics to the physical world. Underlying the study of geometry are basic assumptions about points, lines, and planes. From an understanding of these three terms, other terms and relationships are defined. Further, deductive reasoning—which draws on some basic assumptions to arrive at conclusions—is used in geometry to develop proofs. There are many topics to explore in geometry—from tessellations to topology, from symmetry to spatial visualization.

Initial experiences with geometry do not arise through step-by-step proofs—rather, they come through hands-on explorations of objects in the physical world such as building with blocks or creating three-dimensional objects. From those experiences, an intuitive understanding of how shapes relate to one another and what happens when shapes are combined—a spatial sense—is developed. As explorations continue, the need for a geometric vocabulary to name and identify shapes presents itself in context. These experiences lay the foundation for more formal explorations of geometry, including the properties of polygons and polyhedra (lines, angles, edges, faces, etc.) and their relationships (parallel, perpendicular, congruent, etc.). With experience and an understanding of geometric concepts comes the ability to create convincing arguments and proofs that demonstrate mathematical thinking.

Like number, geometry is linked with other areas of mathematics as well as to other areas of the curriculum. For example, an investigation of tessellations connects to measurement and pattern as well as to art, history, and nature. Geometry also connects mathematics to other disciplines such as architecture, geology, and chemistry.

The GEMS guide *Build It! Festival* provides students with concrete experiences in geometry using two- and three-dimensional shapes. Building with polygons and polyhedra, they develop a geometric vocabulary in context and delve into explorations of pattern, symmetry, congruence and similarity, area, and tessellations. Students also develop spatial sense as they create two- and three-dimensional figures in a variety of ways. Within this GEMS unit, there are pathways for students to investigate concepts at their ability levels and connect with other areas of mathematics. For example, through building several models of the same polygon with varying numbers of pattern blocks, students can explore the concept of equivalence. This same activity can also be used as a springboard into combinatorics, a part of discrete mathematics.

MEASUREMENT

As is the case with geometry, measurement is connected to the real world and is used in everyday life. Measurement appears in many forms and fashions, such as in cooking (uses of both wet and dry measures to prepare recipes), at gas stations (tanks are filled by the gallon, oil is added to cars by quarts), and in daily schedules (clocks and calendars orient us to the date and time of each day). Length, capacity, weight, mass, area, volume, time, temperature, angle, and currency are the main attributes of things in daily life that make use of measurement.

Measurement begins with comparisons—which item is heavier? smaller? longer? wider? To measure real objects and events for comparison, tools are needed. At first, non-standard, familiar items, such as toothpicks or wooden cubes, can be used as a measuring tool. Then, using numbers, the measurements can be quantified, making it possible to compare. Questions—such as How long is each item? Which item is longer? How much longer?—can be answered. Sometimes, non-uniform, non-standard units of measure, such as handspans or feet, are used. These measuring tools often point to the need for a standard unit of measure.

Standard systems of measurement are plentiful: the metric system, English system, currency system, calendar, temperature, and many others. All of these systems allow us to speak a universal language. When someone asks for a yard (or meter) of fabric, the quantity is defined and understood. Likewise, when you order a pound (or kilogram) of coffee, the quantity is understood. When measuring, it is also important to be able to choose the most appropriate unit and tool, and to determine the level of accuracy required for each particular situation.

Measurement is closely connected to geometry through perimeter, area, volume, and angle measurements. In some cases, measurement and geometry also connect to functions—for example, the formulas to determine the area and volume of some geometric figures are functions. Measurement connects to statistics as when comparative data are measured, compared, and analyzed. Both the natural and social sciences also make use of measurement systems.

The GEMS guide *Mother Opossum and Her Babies* includes many measurement activities that use non-standard units. Young students measure a poster of a mother opossum with common classroom items, and use their young opossum models as measurement tools with which to compare objects in the classroom and at home. Many GEMS science guides, including *Height-O-Meters, Experimenting with Model Rockets, Hot Water and Warm Homes from Sunlight,* and *Global Warming* have a key measurement component. Measurement of one kind or another is often crucial to the concept and practice of controlled experimentation.

LOGIC and LANGUAGE

Simply stated, logic is making sense out of something in an organized and reasoned fashion. Logic is used by everyone on a daily basis as they encounter real-world problems. At times, the logic used is very informal such as estimating the number of baskets of strawberries needed for eight adults. At other times, the logic can be more formal and follow a clear strategy or plan such as developing a marketing plan for a new product.

In mathematics, logic includes using reasoning skills, applying strategies, and making valid arguments. It includes all types of problem solving. The methods used to solve problems illustrate different types of logical thinking—from applying a known principle to a new situation to making inferences from everyday experiences. There are many strategies to solve problems including: try something and check it, find a pattern, make an organized list, use manipulatives, draw a picture or diagram, make a table or chart, simplify the problem, do part of the problem, use estimation, make a graph, create models, act it out, work together, work backwards, and use a formula. These strategies are developed over time and to different levels of complexity. Venn diagrams, often utilized in sorting and classification activities, give students an opportunity to organize data logically and explain their classification. Cooperative logic activities, as in the two GEMS *Group Solutions* guides, give students a chance to directly engage in and communicate about increasingly complex logical puzzles.

Language goes hand-in-glove with logic since the thinking and problem solving behind the solutions and arguments needs to be articulated. In many ways, the process of solving a problem is more important than the solution itself. Discussing problems provides opportunities to explain thinking, justify answers, verify and interpret results, draw logical conclusions, make conjectures, and generalize.

Math Around the World is a unit filled with games and activities that have logic and language at their core. In each activity, students use diverse problem-solving skills to determine how to win a game or solve a puzzle. In each case, they are asked to articulate their thinking and explain the strategies involved. Logic and language are also at the very heart of science, forming the basis for the content and methods of scientific reasoning, inquiry, experimentation, and investigation, as well as being necessary for drawing conclusions and communicating findings. The GEMS *Oobleck* unit provides a wonderful example of how logic, language, and what scientists do are inextricably interwoven. In many GEMS guides students use logical thinking and reasoning skills, argue from evidence, draw and refine conclusions, make hypotheses, and design investigations—all grounded in logic and language.

STATISTICS

Data and statistics abound in our lives—from the results of opinion polls regarding the popularity of the President to the amount of rainfall on the weather page of the newspaper. Where does all the information come from and how do we find ways to understand and apply it? Statistics are generated in many ways, including surveys, experiments, sports, polls, demographics, and observations.

The field of statistics involves the collection, classification, analysis, and interpretation of data. Such collections of data are often represented in the form of graphs, tables, or charts. Working with statistics also includes measures of central tendency: mean (average), mode (most frequently occurring number), and median (number that falls in the middle of the numbers listed from lowest to highest). Depending upon what information needs to be conveyed, data can be represented in many different ways. For this reason, careful analysis is needed to judge how the organization of the data impacts the interpretation of that data—especially

the inferences that can be drawn from it. Being able to interpret and understand statistics is a crucially important life skill—particularly in this age of burgeoning technological capabilities that puts so much information at one's fingertips.

Many professionals are dependent upon statistics, including stock brokers, insurance underwriters, public health workers, educators, city planners, product developers, and scientists.

The GEMS guide *Treasure Boxes* provides opportunities for students to use real objects—the treasures—to create concrete graphs. Students record these graphs pictorially or symbolically and make true statements about the graphs as well as pose questions that can be answered by examining the data. In a similar way, *Sifting Through Science* uses concrete graphs to organize the results of science experiments related to buoyancy and magnetism. In *Liquid Explorations* students can graph their favorite drinks, and in *Vitamin C Testing* a graph compares the amounts of Vitamin C the class has found in various juices.

PROBABILITY

Prediction plays an important role in probability. It involves making a guess about something that is expected to happen. Depending upon the amount of prior information, guesses can range from being "wild" to "educated." For example, if asked to predict the outcome of tossing a coin, the two possible outcomes are known—it will either be a head or a tail. This is not a wild guess, but one based on prior information. An understanding of the theoretical probability also helps to make a more informed guess.

Probability is the likelihood that an event will happen. Probability can be expressed numerically, as follows:

$$P(E) \text{ probability of an event} = \frac{\text{number of favorable outcomes}}{\text{total number of possible outcomes}}$$

Applying this to the coin toss, the chances of the coin landing on a head (the "favorable outcome") are one out of two possible outcomes, heads or tails, or (1/2). Similarly, the chances of a tail are one out of two possible outcomes (1/2). Either toss is equally likely to occur. This theoretical probability can be expressed as a fraction, or as a decimal—.5, or as a percentage—50%. The larger the sample of the experimental probability, the closer the results are likely to come to the theoretical probability. Probability can also be measured on a scale from 0 to 1, with 0 representing that an event will never happen, and 1 that it will always happen. The numerical expression of probability links probability to the number strand. Probability is intrinsically connected to statistics as it often involves interpreting data that has been collected and analyzed to determine the likelihood of something happening.

Probability extends into everyday life. Meteorologists try to predict whether it will rain or be sunny based on weather patterns, or they predict where a hurricane will make hit land. Basketball players may be placed by their coach into the game based on their prior shooting statistics and the likelihood that they will shoot at least as well as their average. Consumer product companies survey consumers to determine preferences and then make predictions and plans to alter their product line and advertising for greater profit. People play the lottery and other games of chance hoping to beat the incredible odds against them winning. One bumper sticker went so far as to say: "Lottery: A tax on people who are bad at math."

As its name implies, the GEMS guide *In All Probability* has this subject at its core. Students make predictions about the outcomes of a variety of probability experiments that include a coin toss, two racing games (one using spinners and the other dice), and a more complex Native American game with six two-sided game sticks. These activities provide a context to conduct experiments, gather data, and determine possible outcomes. Students analyze the data and develop an understanding of theoretical probability.

DISCRETE MATHEMATICS

The term discrete mathematics derives from considering mathematical realms that involve separate and countable quantities—*discrete* from each other. This area of mathematics, for example, involves counting principles—delineating things that can be separated from each other and placed into separate ("discrete") groups or categories . Discrete mathematics widens to

include: graph theory (graphs, networks) which use models to analyze data in separate, countable ways; set theory (Venn diagrams, union); combinatorial mathematics (permutations, combinations); game theory (what is the fewest number of moves needed to win) and recurrence relations and iterations (sequences).

Discrete mathematics is used in the real world in many arenas, including: travel routes (from mail carriers to airplane routes to computer circuitry); scheduling delivery routes; organizing tournament schedules that use single elimination to determine the winner; marketing strategies; computer programming; apportionment of seats in Congress; and mortgages. Graph theory, which includes networks, is used to solve problems, such as finding the lowest number of zoo habitats needed for a given number of animals.

Mathematical models are useful tools when working on discrete mathematics problems. For example, charts or diagrams that list the finite, countable number of outcomes to probability problems can be very useful tools to determine theoretical probability. Similarly, charts and diagrams can be used to analyze other types of combinations and permutations. Venn diagrams illustrate the ways that groups of objects are both separate from each other yet also intersect or have some attributes in common. Networks can be drawn to determine if they are able to be traveled, and, if so, whether they are paths or circuits.

Discrete mathematics intersects with many areas of mathematics including number, geometry, statistics, probability, and functions.

The GEMS guide *Math on the Menu* provides students with many opportunities to explore the concept of combinatorics. Students determine the number of combinations possible for a variety of real-world problems such as tostada combinations and color choices for a restaurant. *Math Around the World* presents a series of network problems for students to solve. As they explore problems that have their historical roots in Africa (Shongo Networks) they determine which networks can be traveled and which cannot. The Königsberg Bridge problem is included. Students also delve into investigations related to the breakthrough mathematical work of Euler on paths and circuits.

FUNCTIONS and ALGEBRA

Functions are relationships. There are many types of relationships among quantities, and likewise, there are many ways those relationships can be made explicit. In some cases, a function can be concretely built and described—such as the number of art materials needed for different numbers of people. In other cases, the relationship can be expressed symbolically. For example, $y = 4x$ can be the symbolic representation of the amount of popcorn produced by popping "x" amount of corn kernels as measured in cups. This function represents a proportional relationship between the amount of corn kernels represented by "x" and popcorn represented by "y." These "x" and "y" variables can be organized in what is often called a T-table, and then graphed on a coordinate plane. Since algebra provides the tools to express functions, these two areas of mathematics—functions and algebra—are intertwined.

Cups of corn kernels	Cup of popcorn
0	0
1 / 2	2
1	4
.	.
.	.
.	.
x	4 x

Algebra has been defined as the language of mathematics, or as generalized arithmetic—it provides a way of making the specific universal. Algebra uses variables, operations, and symbolic representation and is often used to describe relationships. Algebra is often perceived as the gateway for students to go on into higher mathematics.

Functions and algebra also connect to other areas of mathematics. In geometry, there is a functional relationship between the area of a triangle and its base and height, or $A = 1/2 (h \times b)$. Likewise, the area of a rectangle is directly related to its length and width and is expressed as $A = L \times W$. Similarly, Euler's formula— $F (faces) + V (vertices) = E (edges) + 2$—expresses the relationship between the number of faces, edges, and vertices of a convex polyhedron. To convert temperatures from one measurement system to another, the formula—$F° = (C° \times 1.8) + 32$—can be applied, given the temperature in either Celsius or Fahrenheit.

Exponential functions, which can be expressed algebraically, have real-world applications. Examples include bacterial growth, radioactive decay, and population growth. There are also many economic applications such as compound interest and maximum profits.

The GEMS guide *Build It! Festival* has an activity in which students explore the relationship between the number of faces, edges, and vertices of regular polyhedron. *Math Around the World* has a puzzle, the Tower of Hanoi, that has exponential growth at its core. By investigating the pattern of moves needed to move disks, students discover that, as the number of disks on the puzzle increases, the number of moves needed to move those disks increases at a rapid rate. *Discovering Density* introduces students to the functional relation between two variables (mass and volume) which determines density, or $D=m/v$. ∎

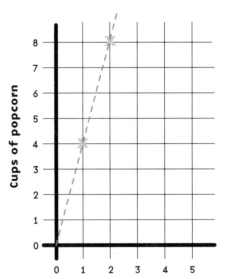

Amount of Popcorn Produced By Popping Corn Kernels In Cups

Appendix B:
Math Strands in GEMS Guides

Note: A (★) means the content area is a major focus in the guide. A (✓) means the content area is represented to a significant extent in the guide, although not a major focus. Please see the front pages and main introductions of each GEMS guide for more detail.

GEMS GUIDES	#	GEO	MEAS	L & L	STAT	PROB	DMATH	F&A	
ACID RAIN	✓		★		✓			✓	
ANIMAL DEFENSES	✓	✓		✓					
ANIMALS IN ACTION				✓					
ANT HOMES UNDER THE GROUND	★			★	✓				
AQUATIC HABITATS	✓		✓		✓				
BUBBLE FESTIVAL	✓	★	★	✓					
BUBBLE-OLOGY	✓	★	★	✓	★			✓	
BUILD IT! FESTIVAL	✓	★	✓	✓				✓	
BUZZING A HIVE	✓	✓		✓					
CHEMICAL REACTIONS	✓		✓					★	
COLOR ANALYZERS									
CONVECTION: A CURRENT EVENT		✓							
CRIME LAB CHEMISTRY				★	✓	✓			
DISCOVERING DENSITY	✓	✓	✓					✓	
DRY ICE INVESTIGATIONS	✓		★	★					
EARTH, MOON, AND STARS		✓	✓						
EARTHWORMS		✓		✓					
EGGS EGGS EVERYWHERE	✓	✓		★	★				
ENVIRONMENTAL DETECTIVES	✓		✓	✓	✓	✓			
EXPERIMENTING WITH MODEL ROCKETS	✓		✓	✓				✓	
FINGERPRINTING		✓		★	✓	✓			
FROG MATH	★	✓		★	★	★	✓		
GLOBAL WARMING	✓		✓		✓				
GROUP SOLUTIONS	★			★					
GROUP SOLUTIONS, TOO!	✓	★		★			✓	✓	
HEIGHT-O-METERS	✓	✓	★					✓	
HIDE A BUTTERFLY		✓							
HOT WATER & WARM HOMES			✓		✓			✓	
IN ALL PROBABILITY	✓			✓	★	★	✓		
INVESTIGATING ARTIFACTS	✓			★	✓		✓		
INVOLVING DISSOLVING	✓		★	✓					
LADYBUGS	✓	✓							
LEARNING ABOUT LEARNING	✓		✓						
LIQUID EXPLORATIONS	✓	✓	✓	✓					
MAPPING ANIMAL MOVEMENTS					★		✓		
MAPPING FISH HABITATS					★		✓		
MATH AROUND THE WORLD	✓			★	✓	✓	✓	✓	
MATH ON THE MENU	★			✓	✓		★	✓	
MESSAGES FROM SPACE	✓		✓	✓		✓			
MICROSCOPIC EXPLORATIONS			★						
MOONS OF JUPITER		✓	✓						
MORE THAN MAGNIFIERS	✓	✓	✓						
MOTHER OPOSSUM AND HER BABIES	★		★	✓					
MYSTERY FESTIVAL			✓	★	✓	✓			
OF CABBAGES AND CHEMISTRY			✓		✓				
ON SANDY SHORES	✓			✓			✓		
OOBLECK		✓							
PAPER TOWEL TESTING	✓		★	✓	★				
PENGUINS AND THEIR YOUNG	★	✓	✓	✓					
QUADICE	★			✓		✓			
RIVER CUTTERS	✓		✓	✓				✓	
SCHOOLYARD ECOLOGY	✓	✓	✓		✓				
SECRET FORMULAS	✓		★	✓				✓	
SIFTING THROUGH SCIENCE	✓	✓		✓	★				
STORIES IN STONE		★							
TERRARIUM HABITATS	✓		✓	✓	✓				
TREASURE BOXES	★	✓		★	★		✓		
TREE HOMES	✓	✓	✓	★					
VITAMIN C TESTING	✓		✓	✓	★			✓	

Appendix C:
GEMS K–5 Math Guides and NCTM Standards

The NCTM Standards for grades K–5 are intrinsic to the GEMS elementary mathematics units. The following list exemplifies how each of the units promotes the standards. It is not intended to be exhaustive, but to demonstrate and briefly describe how these guides make meaningful, age-appropriate, and strong connections to many of the NCTM Standards. **Please note that the new Standards 2000 of the NCTM has further delineated recommendations by grade level, revising the grade level ranges into preK–2, 3–5, 6–8, and 9–12 to promote greater specificity in its recommendations. The GEMS units would also fit well into this new framework, as there are a large number of units in the preschool through second grade range.**

• **Problem Solving.** Problem solving is a key element in all the units and provides the context in which concepts and skills are learned. As students solve different types of problems, they learn and develop strategies they can apply upon encountering new problems. Students are asked thought-provoking questions and have opportunities to explore and investigate possible solutions. The problems posed frequently come from real-world situations and often use materials familiar to the students. Problem solving is a process that permeates all of these GEMS mathematics units (as well as most other GEMS units in both math and science).

Frog Math: As students investigate, sort, classify, graph, estimate, and play games to understand mathematical content, they use problem-solving skills. The Frog Pond game (a version of NIM) has problem solving at its core. In that game, students develop and apply diverse strategies such as making the problem smaller, looking for a pattern, and solving the problem backwards.

Treasure Boxes: The materials used in all of these activities come from the students' world and stimulate problem solving in many arenas—from sorting, classifying, and graphing to determining the best strategy for sharing a given number of objects among a group of people. Students also use problem-solving skills as they locate objects on a coordinate grid.

Group Solutions and **Group Solutions, Too!:** Both of these units focus on using problem solving to find solutions to cooperative logic problems. Throughout, students apply mathematical content knowledge and use deductive reasoning and logical-thinking skills to solve problems.

Math on the Menu: Students encounter a variety of problems in a real-world context that relate to combinatorics, money, geometry, measurement, and number. A variety of strategies can be applied to find solutions to both the routine and non-routine problems.

In All Probability: Students collect data from probability experiments and are asked to organize, represent, and interpret this data. As they set about those tasks, they use problem-solving skills to investigate and understand statistics and probability. Since the activities build on one another, they apply strategies from prior experiences to solve more challenging problems.

Build It! Festival: Whether students construct a three-dimensional shape out of paper models or use pattern blocks to create a symmetrical design, they are actively solving problems related to their physical world. With each activity they learn more about geometry and gain spatial sense.

• **Communication.** Communication plays an important role in each GEMS K–4 mathematics unit. Communication includes, for example, relating concrete materials, pictures, and diagrams to mathematical ideas; reflecting and clarifying thinking about mathematical ideas; relating everyday language to mathematical language and symbols; and understanding that representation, discussion, reading, listening, and writing are vital parts of learning and using mathematics.

Frog Math: Students use concrete materials, such as buttons, plastic frogs, beans, a place value board, dice, and gameboards, to develop mathematical understanding about logic, number, statistics, and probability. They create graphs, have discussions with partners and as a class about the mathematics in the activities, write NIM strategies (Frog Pond game), and gather data to explain the outcome of a probability game (Hop to the Pond).

Treasure Boxes: The real-world objects central to this unit are transformed into mathematical learning tools as they are used to sort and classify, create Venn diagrams and graphs, play a game on a coordinate grid, and divide concretely. Discussion is part of every activity and is done in various formats—in small groups, with a partner, and as a whole class. Journal writing and/or recording is a component of each activity.

Group Solutions and **Group Solutions, Too!:** Without communication, these activities could not be done! As students work cooperatively, they use concrete materials and communicate mathematical information to solve problems. The very nature of cooperative logic involves reading, listening, discussing, explaining, and problem solving. Some problems also lend themselves to recording solutions.

Math on the Menu: Concrete materials are crucial in helping students communicate their solutions to problems—as they find and describe the number of possible tostada combinations and design a restaurant floor plan. Diagrams and pictures also help students to communicate their thinking. As they work with a partner and participate in class discussions, they communicate the underlying mathematics. This is also communicated in a journal that each student keeps to reflect on and clarify their thinking.

In All Probability: Pennies, spinners, markers, dice, game sticks, gameboards, and recording sheets are the "raw" materials students use to collect and represent data. As they are steeped in this process, class discussions help students to reflect and clarify their thinking related to the data. They are also asked to communicate their thinking through graphs and in writing after doing each activity.

Build It! Festival: Concrete materials—including pattern blocks, tangrams, newspaper dowels, paper shapes, and polyhedra—provide the vehicle for students to build representations and communicate their conceptual understanding. Through hands-on experiences and discussion, students learn the vocabulary of geometry, create patterns and tessellations, build symmetrical designs, gain spatial sense, make tangrams, and build three-dimensional shapes.

• **Reasoning.** Reasoning connects to both problem solving and communication, and is also a cornerstone of each of the GEMS K–4 units. The reasoning students use allows them to reach logical conclusions. To explain their reasoning, they can use models, known facts, properties, and relationships. In addition, they use patterns and relationships to analyze mathematical situations. Using reasoning, students should be able to explain their solutions and justify their answers. Ultimately, reasoning allows students to see that mathematics truly makes sense!

Frog Math: Students have to explain their reasoning in the following ways: how buttons are sorted; what the graph communicates; whether or not it is important to go first or second in the Frog Pond game; how to capture the "magic" frog; and why some frogs in the Hop to the Pond game win more often than other frogs.

Treasure Boxes: Reasoning comes into play as students make and explain Venn diagrams, create graphs complete with "true statements," and generate related questions. Students also explain how they divided treasure, discussing what is the best method and why, and they use a coordinate grid to locate objects in a logical fashion.

Group Solutions and **Group Solutions, Too!:** Students delineate their reasoning and justify their "group solution" by reviewing the clue cards and explaining the reasoning involved in the solution.

Math on the Menu: As students solve a variety of combination problems, they can use models, charts, and patterns to explain and justify their solutions. They can also draw on prior solutions to apply what they've learned to reach a logical answer. Using a model of a restaurant, they can explain how they designed its components. In all the activities, as students are asked to explain their thinking and justify their answers, other students learn reasoning skills from their peers.

In All Probability: Using collected data, known facts (such as the 36 possible outcomes of rolling two dice in the horse race game), and their reasoning skills, students explain the outcomes for each of the probability games. Students can also apply the thinking and reasoning behind the outcome of the penny toss to explain the outcomes of Native American game sticks.

Build It! Festival: As students analyze patterns, they can determine "What Comes Next" in a sequence or build a tessellation. They also create informal "proofs" to explain geometric concepts based on their experience with concrete models of two- and three-dimensional shapes.

• **Connections.** When students are given opportunities to make connections within the various areas of mathematics, they can link conceptual understanding and procedural knowledge; relate various representations of concepts/procedures to one another; and identify relationships among the different topics. Additionally, we want students to see that mathematics connects to other curricular areas and is used in our daily lives.

Frog Math: This unit takes advantage of meaningful literature connections that relate button sorts to graphing and data collection to understanding chance. Students apply number sense to each activity. Other connections to literature are rich in mathematical content.

Treasure Boxes: The activities relate treasure sorts to graphing, coordinate grids to real-world maps, and sharing to division. Students apply number sense to each activity and the connections to literature are strong in mathematical content.

Group Solutions and **Group Solutions, Too!:** Students draw on knowledge of other areas of mathematics—including number sense, geometry, and graphing—to solve problems. They work cooperatively toward solutions to problems which helps prepare for real-world workplaces. Activities model positive ways to work through social and citizenship issues.

Math on the Menu: As students solve combination problems related to tostadas and combination plates for a restaurant, their number sense comes into play, as well as their use of money in context, to determine the cost of each combination. The activities are connected to the real-world situation of a restaurant and students create floor plans using geometry and measurement skills.

In All Probability: The activities involve application of number sense to data collection, and representation to understanding chance (probability). Students evaluate graphs from newspapers and magazines and the unit connects to other real-world aspects of probability such as games of chance, raffles, the lottery, etc.

Build It! Festival: This unit connects two- and three-dimensional geometry to the real world—everything has shape and form. The unit makes real-world connections to symmetry, patterns, and tessellations. Activities also make connections to art and architecture.

• **Number Sense and Numeration.** To develop number sense and numeration skills, students need to construct number meanings through real-world experiences and the use of physical materials; need to understand our numeration system by relating counting, grouping, and place value concepts; and need to interpret numbers in the many ways they are encountered in the real world.

Frog Math: Numbers are used to sort and graph buttons, to interpret sorts, graphs and data collection. After students make "guesstimations," they use a place value board for counting the actual number of items in those estimations. Students also use numbers in context as they roll dice and play the Hop to the Pond games.

Treasure Boxes: Students use numbers to sort and graph real-world objects, to interpret sorts, and create Venn diagrams. Number recognition and counting skills are also used in the Treasure Map activity, and the sharing activities involve counting "fair shares" in a variety of ways, including by 1's, 2's, 5's, and 10's, which lays the foundation for division.

Group Solutions and **Group Solutions, Too!:** All the activity families in these units involve use of number sense to solve problems.

Math on the Menu: Students use number sense to determine the finite number of combinations possible, as well as solve problems using the monetary system.

In All Probability: Data collection and making sense of data involve an understanding and application of number sense. The use of dice, spinners, and game sticks in games requires understanding of numbers in a real-world context.

Build It! Festival: Numbers are used in relation to shapes and their geometric properties.

• **Geometry and Spatial Sense.** To develop an understanding of two- and three-dimensional geometry and spatial sense, students need to: describe, model, draw, and classify shapes; investigate and predict the results of combining, subdividing, and changing shapes; relate geometric ideas to number and measurement; and recognize and appreciate geometry in their world.

Frog Math: The shape of buttons is used as an attribute to sort, classify, and graph. Dice (hexahedrons) are used in a real-world context.

Treasure Boxes: The shapes of real-world objects are used to sort, classify, and graph. A coordinate grid is used to play a game.

Group Solutions and **Group Solutions, Too!:** Knowledge of shapes is applied to solve logic problems. In the second volume application of geometry and spatial sense is a major focus of the "What's Cookin'?" and "Get Into Shapes" activity families.

Math on the Menu: As students design restaurant layout plans, they use spatial sense and two-dimensional geometric models of real-world objects.

Build It! Festival: The essence of this unit is geometric understanding and spatial sense. Students use pattern blocks, tangrams, newspaper dowels, paper models, and polyhedra to learn geometric vocabulary and concepts and to gain spatial sense. Relevant connections to their world are made throughout the unit.

• **Statistics and Probability.** To develop the ability to analyze data and gain an understanding of probability, students need to: collect, organize, and describe data; construct, read, and interpret displays of data; formulate and solve problems that involve collecting and analyzing data; and explore the concept of chance.

Frog Math: Students collect and organize data as they sort and graph. They also gather data on handfuls of beans and organize the data to interpret the results (looking for an "average"). Students use dice to explore the concept of chance as they play the Hop to the Pond games. By keeping track of the outcomes, they discuss the "fairness" of the game based on data.

Treasure Boxes: Activities include data collection and organization through sorting and graphing. In particular, students focus on "true statements" about the data on their graphs. The concept of chance is informally explored in the Hidden Treasure game.

Group Solutions, Too!: The "More Searches" activity family includes the interpretation of graphs.

Math on the Menu: Determining the number of possible combinations for tostadas, combination plates, and color schemes requires organization of information to be sure all possible combinations are determined. The cost analysis of ingredients to determine a price to charge involves data analysis.

In All Probability: The essence of this unit is probability and statistics. Students collect, organize, analyze, and interpret data in all activities. Pennies, dice, spinners, and game sticks are used to explore chance. The knowledge students gain in the unit is applied to graphs from the real world.

Build It! Festival: Students collect data to determine how many ways a polygon can be filled with pattern blocks. Tangram pieces are used to create real-world shapes and many different polygons. As polygons are created, recorded data describes and keeps track of all possibilities. ■

Appendix D: More on the NCTM Standards

In 1989, the National Council of Teachers of Mathematics (NCTM) published *Curriculum and Evaluation Standards for School Mathematics.* In 1991, the NCTM issued *Professional Standards for Teaching Mathematics,* and in 1995 *Assessment Standards for School Mathematics.* These three publications were sometimes referred to collectively as "The Standards." Although the rainbow/raindrop/sun metaphor and the math content strands we've selected for GEMS have their own unique character and differ somewhat in nomenclature and emphasis, they are compatible with and can be very closely aligned to these NCTM standards—sharing fundamental ideas as regards content, pedagogy, equity, real-world connections, and many other elements of modern mathematics instruction. In 2000, the NCTM published *Principles and Standards for School Mathematics.* This document blended the contents of the two earlier standards and describes a vision of mathematics education that includes: principles for school mathematics; standards for mathematics education for grades PK through grade 12; and the steps to move toward the vision of these Principles and Standards. The Principles and Standards for School Mathematics address the following overarching themes: Equity; Curriculum; Teaching; Learning; Assessment; and Technology. The Mathematics Standards for all grade levels include: (1) Number and Operation; (2) Algebra; (3) Geometry (4) Measurement; (5) Data Analysis and Probability; (6) Problem Solving; (7) Reasoning and Proof; (8) Communication; (9) Connections; and (10) Representation. Many of these standards are referred to in this handbook's discussion of the GEMS K–5 mathematics guides, as well as in the more detailed summary of these guides in Appendix C. There are also evaluation standards.

This new document is designed to build on the original NCTM Standards documents, consolidate the classroom aspects of all three documents, and, based on extensive research, comment, and collaborative discussion, propose major directions in mathematics education for the new century.

Importantly, the document also revises the grade level ranges into preK–2, 3–5, 6–8, and 9–12 to promote greater specificity in its recommendations.

The introduction to *Principles and Standards* stresses that ours is a time of "extraordinary and accelerating change" with the world "dramatically different from what it was in 1989." Greatly increased student access to computers and the World Wide Web is cited as one key example, and the document points out that "school mathematics education bears increasing responsibilities in a data-rich era." Technology is an important emphasis. The introduction also articulates five "guiding principles" for school mathematics programs. These are: The Equity Principle (mathematics instructional programs should promote the learning of mathematics by *all* students); The Mathematics Curriculum Principle (mathematics instructional programs should emphasize important and meaningful mathematics through curricula that are coherent and comprehensive); The Teaching Principle (mathematics instructional programs depend on competent and caring teachers who teach all students to understand and use mathematics; The Learning Principle (mathematics instructional programs should enable students to understand and use mathematics); The Assessment Principle (mathematics instructional programs should include assessment to monitor, enhance, and evaluate the mathematics learning of all students and to inform teaching); and The Technology Principle (mathematics instructional programs should use technology to help all students understand mathematics and should prepare them to use mathematics in an increasingly technological world.

This document can be found and downloaded from **www.nctm.org** in a convenient electronic edition or can be ordered from the NCTM, 1906 Association Drive, Reston VA 20191. Underlying all their work is the NCTM "Statement of Beliefs," which appears below:

As the primary professional organization for teachers of mathematics in grades K–12, the National Council of Teachers of Mathematics (NCTM) has the responsibility to provide broad national leadership in matters related to mathematics education. In meeting this responsibility, NCTM has developed a set of standards for school mathematics that address content, teaching, and assessment. These standards are guidelines for teachers, schools, districts, states, and provinces to use in planning, implementing, and evaluating high-quality mathematics programs for kindergarten through grade 12.

The NCTM Standards are based on a set of core beliefs about students, teaching, learning, and mathematics. We believe the following:

• Every student deserves an excellent program of instruction in mathematics that challenges each student to achieve at the high level required for productive citizenship and employment.

• Every student must be taught by qualified teachers who have a sound knowledge of mathematics and how children learn mathematics and who also hold high expectations for themselves and their students.

• Each school district must develop a complete and coherent mathematics curriculum that focuses, at every grade level, on the development of numerical, algebraic, geometric, and statistical concepts and skills that enable all students to formulate, analyze, and solve problems proficiently. Teachers at every grade level should understand how the mathematics they teach fits into the development of these strands.

• Computational skills and number concepts are essential components of the mathematics curriculum, and a knowledge of estimation and mental computation are more important than ever. By the end of the middle grades, students should have a solid foundation in number, algebra, geometry, measurement, and statistics.

• Teachers guide the learning process in their classrooms and manage the classroom environment through a variety of instructional approaches directly tied to the mathematics content and to students' needs.

• Learning mathematics is maximized when teachers focus on mathematical thinking and reasoning. Progressively more formal reasoning and mathematical proof should be integrated into the mathematics program as a student continues in school.

• Learning mathematics is enhanced when content is placed in context and is connected to other subject areas and when students are given multiple opportunities to apply mathematics in meaningful ways as part of the learning process.

• The widespread impact of technology on nearly every aspect of our lives requires changes in the content and nature of school mathematics programs. In keeping with these changes, students should be able to use calculators and computers to investigate mathematical concepts and increase their mathematical understanding.

• Students use diverse strategies and different algorithms to solve problems, and teachers must recognize and take advantage of these alternative approaches to help students develop a better understanding of mathematics.

• The assessment of mathematical understanding must be aligned with the content taught and must incorporate multiple sources of information, including standardized tests, quizzes, observations, performance tasks, and mathematical investigations.

• The improvement of mathematics teaching and learning should be guided by ongoing research and by ongoing assessment of school mathematics programs.

• Changing mathematics programs in ways that reflect these beliefs requires collaborative efforts and ongoing discussions among all the stakeholders in the process. NCTM stands ready to work with all those who care about improving mathematics education for all students. Through such dialogue and cooperative efforts, we can improve the mathematical competence of the students in mathematics classes across the continent.

Appendix E:
Bibliography and Helpful Web Links

American Association for the Advancement of Science, *Science for All Americans*, Oxford University Press, New York/Oxford, 1990.

California State Department of Education, *Mathematics Framework for California Public Schools*, 1985.

Grouws (editor), *Handbook of Research on Mathematics Teaching and Learning,* Macmillan Publishing Company, New York, 1992.

Langbort and Thompson, *Building Success in Math*, Dale Seymour, White Plains, New York, 1985.

National Council of Teachers of Mathematics, *Curriculum and Evaluation Standards for School Mathematics*, Reston, Virginia, 1989.

National Council of Teachers of Mathematics, *Professional Standards for Teaching Mathematics*, Reston, Virginia, 1991.

National Council of Teachers of Mathematics, *Principles and Standards for School Mathematics,* Reston, Virginia, 2000.

National Research Council, *Everybody Counts: A Report to the Nation on the Future of Mathematics Education*, National Academy Press, Washington, D.C., 1989.

National Research Council, *National Science Education Standards*, National Academy Press, Washington, D.C., 1996.

NSTA Pathways to the Science Standards: *Guidelines for Moving the Vision into Practice* (elementary edition), National Science Teacher's Association, Arlington, Virginia, 1997.

Oakes*, Multiplying Inequalities: The Effects of Race, Social Class, and Tracking on Opportunities to Learn Mathematics and Science*, Rand Corporation, Santa Monica, 1990.

Shoenfeld, *Mathematical Problem Solving*, Academic Press, New York, 1985.

Skolnick, Langbort, and Day, *How to Encourage Girls in Math and Science,* Prentice Hall, Englewood Cliffs, New Jersey, 1982.

Trentacosta & Kenney (editors) *Multicultural and Gender Equity in The Mathematics Classroom: The Gift of Diversity,* NCTM, National Council of Teachers of Mathematics, Reston, Virginia 1997.

Some Mathematics on the World Wide Web

National Council of Teachers of Mathematics' Web site
http://www.nctm.org/

The Eisenhower National Clearinghouse for mathematics and science education.
http://enc.org/

Lawrence Hall of Science
http://www.lhs.berkeley.edu/GEMS

History of mathematics—biographies, chronologies and lots more.
http://www-groups.dcs.st-and.ac.uk:80/~history/

Women mathematicians
http://www.scottlan.edu/lriddle/women/women.htm

Stories/activities for K-12 students, from Los Alamos National Laboratory.
http://www.c3.lanl.gov/mega-math/

Plane Math—math and aeronautics
http://www.planemath.com/

Interactive Mathematics Online
http://tqd.advanced.org/2647/index.html

The Fractory teaches about fractals
http://tqd.advanced.org/3288/

Eric's Treasure Trove of Mathematics: excellent reference.
http://www.gps.caltech.edu/~eww/math/math.html

Project ARISE, a mathematics pilot program, taught in a real-world context.
http://www.napanet.net/~jlege/

MathMania—knots, graphs, sorting networks, and more
http://csr.uvic.ca/~mmania/

PBS Mathline: elementary, middle and high school math projects.
http://www.pbs.org/learn/mathline/

The Math Forum—Ask Dr. Math: an interactive Q&A
http://forum.swarthmore.edu/dr.math/

The Geometry Center, includes Java applications
http://www.geom.umn.edu/welcome.html

The Mathematics Archives, classified into five main categories, searchable
http://archives.math.utk.edu/

Introduction

1. Think back to when you went to school—what were your math experiences like?

2. In the past, math class often meant computational skills alone. Times have changed. Mathematics programs need to reflect these changes by broadening the scope of what we teach to develop mathematically powerful students.

3. This presentation uses the metaphor of a rainbow to portray modern mathematics education.

NUMBER
Project the first overhead (or put up first felt arc labeled "Number" in middle of felt board.

1. Computational skills are still an important part of every student's tool kit. But number is much more than computation.

2. Students need conceptual understanding about number. Numbers are quantifiers—they tell us how much and how many.

3. Estimation, place value, and number theory are all also part of this strand.

4. Number plays a very basic and integral role in all of mathematics and is interwoven through all the strands, but mathematics is also much more than number. Let's continue creating the rainbow by adding:

GEOMETRY
Place felt arc labeled "Geometry."

1. Everything has a shape or a form that is either two- or three-dimensional. If we look around the room, we can see many examples of geometric shapes.

2. Many of us remember geometry from high school with two-column proofs. But geometry explorations need to start in the early grades with concrete experiences.

3. Geometry connects mathematics to many other disciplines (art. architecture, geology, chemistry, etc.)

MEASUREMENT
Place felt arc labeled "Measurement."

1. Measurement interweaves naturally with both number and geometry.

2. Measuring involves more than using a tool and getting a number for an answer. It also involves decisions about accuracy and interpreting the measurement.

3. Measurement is used in all occupations and in everyday life (time, cooking or ordering food, gas in car, etc.).

LOGIC and LANGUAGE
Place felt arc labeled "Logic and Language."

1. Logic is a fundamental thinking skill that allows us to make sense out of things—a skill we use every day.

2. Students need to develop a repertoire of problem-solving strategies that allow them to think in creative ways to solve complex problems.

3. Some problems have multiple solutions. Beyond solving the problem, students should be able to explain their logic and reasoning.

4. Logic and language intersects with all other strands and with science, writing, social studies, and literature.

STATISTICS
Place felt arc labeled "Statistics"

1. From cereal box to sports pages, we are presented with information in the form of data.

2. Students need experience with data—collecting, organizing, and creating representations for data in the form of graphs.

3. All of us—students and adults alike—need to use critical thinking skills to determine the validity of the data, and to evaluate its presentation and interpretation.

4. The work of many professionals depends on statistics (including stockbrokers, city planners. insurance underwriters, etc.).

PROBABILITY
Place felt arc labeled "Probability."

1. What is probability?—The likelihood of an event occurring, the chance that something will or will not happen. Often we predict outcomes about what is likely to happen.

2. Give example of flipping a penny. The theoretical probability of the penny flip is 1 out of 2, and can be expressed in fractions, decimals, or percentages. The experimental probability is what happens when we actually start flipping the penny—which does not always match the theoretical probability! (Over time, as the number of flips increases, the experimental probability more closely approximates the theoretical.)

3. Students begin to understand probability by conducting probability experiments—often in the form of games, using spinners and dice.

4. Meterologists and seismologists use statistics and probability in their work.

5. Probability is closely connected with both statistics and number. It also connects to the next strand.

DISCRETE MATHEMATICS
Place felt arc labeled "Discrete Mathematics."

1. The word discrete means separate and distinct. In mathematics, it refers to separate and countable quantities versus continuous quantities.
Some examples: sugar cubes vs. pouring honey; going down steps vs. going down a slide.

2. One area of discrete mathematics is systematic listing and counting. Example: three hats and four pairs of sunglasses, how many different combinations of one hat and one pair of glasses? Combinatorics is also a part of discrete mathematics.

3. Discrete mathematics includes graph theory. Some real-world examples are travel routes, schedules for tournaments, and frequencies for radio stations.

4. Looking for an optimal solution, such as the fewest number of moves in a strategic game, also is part of discrete mathematics.

FUNCTIONS and ALGEBRA
Place felt arc labeled "Functions and Algebra."

1. Functions are relationships. Example: the relationship between the number of people and their total number of eyes.

2. More complex functions are relationships between two or more things and can often be expressed as a formula, such as: area of a rectangle = l x w. Many functions can be expressed algebraically.

3. Algebra is the language of mathematics, or generalized arithmetic. It uses variables, operations, and symbolic representation. It expresses the relationship among quantities in a general form.

4. Primary students can explore algebra informally with concrete materials (such as doing missing addend problems with bear counters).

5. To further develop their abilities, students need opportunities to represent number patterns with tables and graphs, verbalize rules, and create equations.

Stress that:

All of these strands are meant to be part of math programs for all students, at all grade levels. In the early years, a foundation is laid on which to build deeper understandings and skills in later grades.

Raindrops: Tools and Strategies

The raindrops represent tools and strategies for making mathematics come alive in the classroom.

The first raindrop is **TOOLS**
Add second overhead (or put the "Tool" raindrop on the felt board).

Mathematical tools include concrete materials, such as pattern blocks, dice, and cubes, as well as calculators and computers.

This next raindrop is…**DISCOURSE**
Put the "Discourse" raindrop on the felt board.

Discourse refers to the communication of mathematics, facilitated by the teacher, in a classroom environment that fosters learning by all students.

COLLABORATION
Put the "Collaboration" raindrop on the felt board.

The ability to work together and solve problems collaboratively—where everyone's ideas are part of the process—is all-important in the workplace.

REAL-WORLD PROBLEMS AND INVESTIGATIONS
Put the "Real-World Problems and Investigations" raindrop on the felt board.

Problems that connect with real-world experiences are an important entry point to engage students in looking for solutions. Some problems require rigorous work and go beyond the classroom for solutions or information—these are **investigations.**

AUTHENTIC ASSESSMENT
Put the "Authentic Assessment" raindrop on the felt board.

Assessment needs to align with curriculum and instruction.

The Sun and Its Rays

Add third overhead (or put the "Sun" on the felt board).

The Sun represents the K–8 curriculum. The rays are overarching parts of the curriculum that need to be a central focus as teachers present content with appropriate teaching practices.

PATTERNS
Put the "Patterns" ray on the felt board.

A pattern can be found in anything that repeats itself over and over. Finding, making, and extending patterns is fundamental to mathematics.

PROBLEM SOLVING

Put the "Problem Solving" ray on the felt board.

In addition to being an ability students need to develop, problem solving is an overall process that permeates the curriculum—the context in which concepts and skills can be learned.

COMMUNICATION

Put the "Communication" ray on the felt board.

Communication provides a way for students to explain what they have learned, reflect on ideas, clarify thinking and collaborate effectively with each other.

REASONING

Put the "Reasoning" ray on the felt board.

Mathematics is reasoning—we cannot do math without it. Students need to gain confidence in their ability to reason and to justify their thinking.

CONNECTIONS

Put the "Connections" ray on the felt board.

None of the topic areas in the rainbow are meant to be taught in isolation—they are connected. Mathematics also connects to other subject areas and to real-life.

Pots of Gold

The pots of gold represent:

MATH POWER

FOR ALL STUDENTS

Add fourth overhead (or place pots of gold on the felt board).

Mathematics education programs should develop students' abilities and their confidence, meeting the needs of all students regardless of background, gender, language, learning or physical challenges.

Conclusion

This rainbow metaphor reflects the richness of modern mathematics education and its connection to science, technology, other fields of study, and the real world. Through the work of teachers and educators, with active parent involvement , all students should have the chance to gain mathematical power. In this way, the rainbow of mathematics will be transformed from vision to reality.

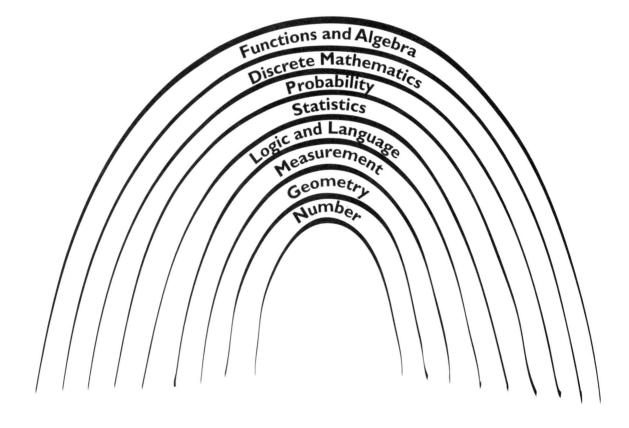

Functions and Algebra

Discrete Mathematics

Probability

Statistics

Logic and Language

Measurement

Geometry

Number

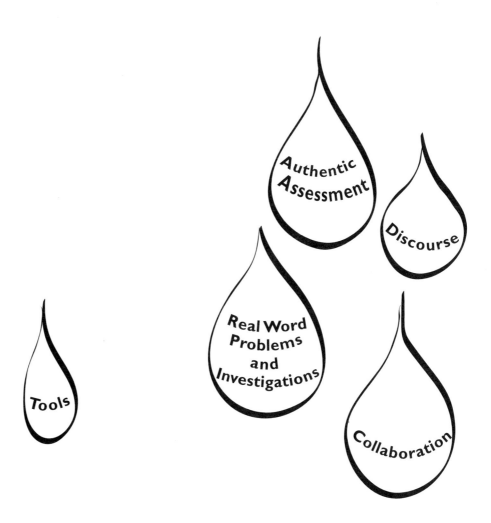

Authentic Assessment

Discourse

Real Word Problems and Investigations

Collaboration

Tools

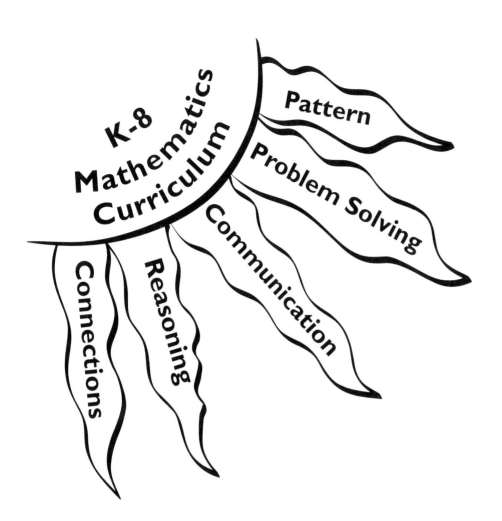

K-8
Mathematics
Curriculum

Pattern

Problem Solving

Communication

Reasoning

Connections

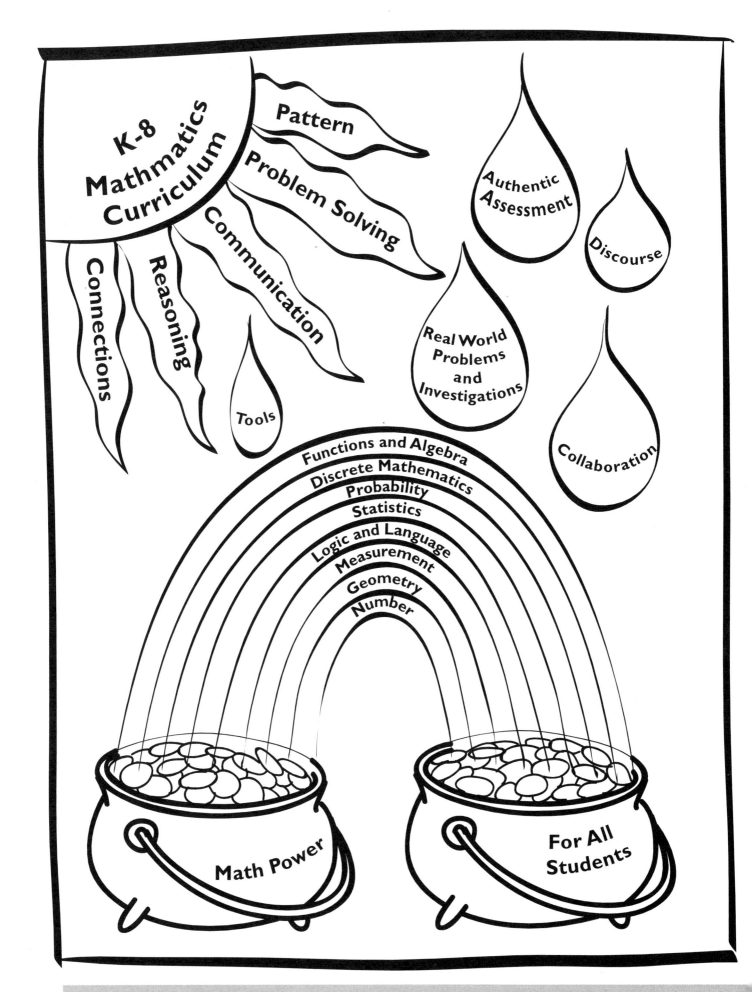